COMMON
LECTIONARY:

The Lectionary Proposed
by the
Consultation on Common Texts

The Church Hym
800 Second Avenue,

10   9   8   7   6   5   4   3

Contents

Acknowledgments

Common Lectionary: The Lectionary Proposed by the Consultation on Common Texts ©1983, James M. Schellman.

"The Bible text in this publication is from the Revised Standard Version Bible, Catholic Edition, copyrighted 1965 and 1966 by the Division of Christian Education of the National Council of Churches of Christ in the U.S.A., and used by permission."

Excerpt reprinted from *Church Dogmatics I/1, The Doctrine of the Word of God* by Karl Barth and tr. by G. T. Thomson 1936, T & T Clark, Edinburgh. Used with permission.

Excerpt from Lucien Deiss, C.S.Sp., *Springtime of the Liturgy* 1979, by the Order of St. Benedict, Inc., published by The Liturgical Press, Collegeville, Minnesota. Used with permission.

Excerpt reprinted by permission from *Psalms: The Prayer Book of the Bible* by Dietrich Bonhoeffer and tr. by James H. Burtness 1970, Augsburg Publishing House.

Excerpt from *The Book of Common Prayer* Copyright 1977 by Charles Mortimer Guilbert as Custodian of the Standard Book of Common Prayer. All rights reserved.

Excerpt reprinted from "The Lectionary as a Context for Interpretation" by Gerard S. Sloyan in *Interpretation: A Journal of Bible and Theology*, Union Theological Seminary, 31/2 (April, 1979). Used with permission.

Foreword

With this publication the Consultation on Common Texts (CCT) presents to the Churches its *Common Lectionary*. This lectionary represents a conservative harmonization of the major variants of the three-year lectionary used at this time in North America.

The *Common Lectionary* was released by the CCT to the Churches at the beginning of 1983 for a three-year trial period ending 1 December 1986. At the conclusion of this trial period the CCT will consider recommendations received from the Churches and will make revisions as appropriate in the lectionary. The final version of the *Common Lectionary* will then be released to the Churches in 1987.

The contents of this publication are as follows:

Introduction: The introduction provides a full description of the three-year lectionary and of the principles and goals of the *Common Lectionary* in particular. It is essential to read the introduction before evaluating this lectionary.

Table of Readings and Psalms: This table contains the citations for the Scripture selections that constitute the *Common Lectionary*. The versification follows that given in the *Revised Standard Version*. The psalms follow the Hebrew numbering. Parentheses within Scripture citations indicate verses that may be added or subtracted depending upon homiletical intent and pastoral need.

List of Titles: This list contains the titles used in the *Common Lectionary* for the seasons, Sundays, and special days of the liturgical year. For the Sundays that follow Pentecost, the Episcopal system of "Propers" has been adopted and combined with the United Methodist system of giving inclusive dates for each of these Sundays.

Comparative List of Titles: This list contains the titles given to each Sunday by the several denominational lectionaries used in North America. This list will aid those who wish to compare the recommendations of the *Common Lectionary* for a particular day with the Scripture assigned to that day in their denominational lectionary. For example, by consulting this list an evaluator will be able to see that Proper 16 in the *Common Lectionary* is the Fourteenth Sunday after Pentecost in the *Lutheran Book of Worship* and the Twenty-first

Sunday in Ordinary Time in the Roman Catholic *Ordo Lectionum Missae.*

Explanatory Notes for Year A, Year B, Year C, and Special Days: These notes provide evaluators with background information on the decisions reached regarding the readings and psalms assigned to each Sunday in the *Common Lectionary*. They will be especially helpful to those wishing to compare this lectionary with their denominational systems.

Index of Scripture: This is an index of the readings and psalms contained in the *Common Lectionary.*

Questionnaire: This questionnaire is for the use of congregations and individuals that take part in the evaluation of the *Common Lectionary.* In the case of evaluation by congregations or groups, it would be especially helpful if a single questionnaire representing the evaluation of the group could be prepared. Ideally this would involve the use of the readings and psalms at worship and subsequent discussion by a number of those involved: leaders/preachers, readers, other members of the congregation. Completed questionnaires may be sent to denominational offices, for subsequent forwarding to the CCT, or directly to the secretariat of the CCT:

Consultation on Common Texts
1234 Massachusetts, Ave. N.W., Suite 1009
Washington, D.C. 20005

Those participating in the evaluation of the *Common Lectionary* may reproduce for this purpose individual sections of this publication (for example, introduction, table, and questionnaire). The full contents of the publication may not be reproduced.

Introduction

Of the gifts of the Second Vatican Council to the Church catholic the Roman Lectionary of 1969 must be accounted as one of the foremost.[1] It was the direct result of a declaration in the Constitution on the Liturgy to the effect that

> The treasures of the Bible are to be opened up more lavishly, so that a richer share in God's word may be provided for the faithful. In this way a more representative portion of holy Scripture will be read to the people in the course of a prescribed number of years.[2]

The second edition (1981) of that Lectionary reiterates that mandate and specifies its liturgical context:

> In the celebration of the liturgy the word of God is not voiced in only one way nor does it always stir the hearts of the hearers with the same power. Always, however, Christ is present in his word; as he carries out the mystery of salvation, he sanctifies us and offers the Father perfect worship.
>
> Moreover, the word of God unceasingly calls to mind and extends the plan of salvation, which achieves its fullest expression in the liturgy. The liturgical celebration becomes therefore the continuing, complete, and effective presentation of God's word.
>
> That word constantly proclaimed in the liturgy is always, then, a living, active word through the power of the Holy Spirit. It expresses the Father's love that never fails in its effectiveness toward us.[3]

The formative conciliar document specifies that

> The two parts that, in a certain sense, go to make up the Mass, namely, the liturgy of the word and the liturgy of the eucharist, are so closely connected with each other that they form but one single act of worship.[4]

This liturgical context of the word of God has been given explicit expression by Fr. Gaston Fontaine, C.R.I.C., Secretary to the working body, *Coetus XI*,[5] which produced the *Ordo Lectionum Missae*:

> If the celebration of the liturgy is not the only place where we are nourished by the divine Word, it has nevertheless a privileged posi-

tion. The proclamation of Scripture within the context of the community gathered for worship is itself an assurance of Christ's presence. The liturgy of the word and the liturgy of the eucharist, "so closely connected with each other that they form but one single act of worship," makes us sharers in the faith of Christ crucified and risen and, through him who is the crown of it all, causes us to enter more fully into the whole historic work of salvation.[6]

The wisdom embodied in the work of Coetus XI, now in universal use in the churches that follow the Roman rite, has been attested by a completely unexpected and salutary development, particularly in North America, but also in other parts of the world. That is the appropriation of the Roman Lectionary by more than a few Protestant and Anglican churches. This process began with the publication in 1970 of an edition thereof in *The Worshipbook*,[7] a service book and hymnal jointly produced by three Presbyterian churches in the United States. Shortly thereafter the Episcopal and Lutheran churches included it in preliminary studies[8] which resulted in its inclusion in the *Draft Proposed Book of Common Prayer*[9] and subsequently adopted *Book of Common Prayer*,[10] and also the *Lutheran Book of Worship*.[11] In the meantime the United Methodist Church in the U.S.A. made an edition available in 1976[12] and the Disciples of Christ as well as the United Church of Christ in the U.S.A. adopted for voluntary use the Presbyterian version. These developments were materially assisted by the publication of a consensus edition in pamphlet form by the ecumenical Consultation on Church Union, representing (at that time) nine Protestant denominations seeking fuller unity.[13]

In Canada the United Church has undertaken an experimental use of the three-year lectionary in a number of parishes, and the Anglican Church has published a pamphlet (1981)[14] making it available. This step was in keeping with a resolution of the 1978 Lambeth Conference of Bishops of the Anglican churches throughout the world which declared:

> The Conference recommends a common lectionary for the Eucharist and the Offices as a unifying factor within our Communion and ecumenically; and draws attention to the experience of those Provinces which have adopted the three year Eucharistic lectionary of the Roman Catholic Church.[15]

Although this widespread ecumenical use of the Roman Lectionary is almost unique to the North American continent it is nevertheless eloquent testimony to the dedication and thoroughness with which the will of the Second Vatican Council was carried forward. It has also provided a dimension of ecumenical experience which is as effective as it has been unexpected. In countless towns, villages and urban parish neighborhoods groups of clergy and laity, Catholic, Anglican, and Protestant, are meeting each week to work exegetically and pastorally with the readings for the approaching Sunday. In some places congregations of different denominations are jointly supporting the ministry of a church musician who, by working with the lectionary, may provide similar musical contributions to the liturgy of those churches.

A further evidence of the extensive use of *Ordo Lectionum Missae* in its various denominational adaptations has been the appearance of an entire array of exegetical and homiletical publications based thereon. Commentaries on the whole three-year set of lessons have been prepared by such scholars as Reginald H. Fuller (originally printed in *Worship* magazine)[16] and Gerard Sloyan.[17] The Fortress Press has produced an impressive series of paperbacks covering each season of the church year and, more recently, whole books of the Bible, the "Proclamation" series. Numerous weekly homiletical services may be subscribed to such as that of the Liturgical Conference of Washington, D.C.

Responding to this important liturgical ecumenism, the (North American) Consultation on Common Texts (CCT) convened in Washington, D.C. a conference attended by representatives of thirteen churches in the United States and Canada, March 29-31, 1978. The purpose was to assess the usefulness of the Roman Lectionary and to determine what steps, if any, should be taken in terms of harmonization and revision. The Consultation (CCT) itself originated in the mid-1960's in an attempt to provide commonly-accepted English texts for the Lord's Prayer, the creeds, canticles, and invariable prayers of the Mass.[18] One of its founders also convened the Washington conference, the Rev. Prof. Massey H. Shepherd, Jr., of the Episcopal Church. Present as specially invited participants were Fr. Fontaine, Secretary of Coetus XI, the Rev. Prof. Reginald Fuller, and the Rev. Prof. James F. White of the United Methodist Church, then President of the North American Academy of Liturgy.

Minutes of the conference record that "the representatives voted unanimously that they desired closer unity and as much consensus as possible with the three-year lectionary."[19] They agreed on a calendar, on the need for a commonly-accepted schedule of psalmody, and on certain terminology. In particular they recommended to the Consultation on Common Texts that it set up a small working body to produce a consensus table of readings which would revise the present Old Testament selections in the Sunday cycle

> in order to provide readings that are more completely representative
> of the Hebrew Bible and not simply prophetic or typological; this
> includes the possibility of aligning the Old Testament passage with
> the New Testament selection rather than with the Gospel.[20]

The Consultation on Common Texts proceeded to set up the North American Committee on Calendar and Lectionary (NACCL). Its Chair has been the Rev. Dr. Lewis A. Briner, a minister of the United Presbyterian Church. He described the work of the Committee in 1980 as "resolving the differences now evident in lectionary patterns and . . . insuring a less typological use of the Old Testament, alongside Epistle and Gospel readings."[21] Membership on the Committee has included pastors and scholars from the Roman Catholic, Episcopal, Presbyterian, Lutheran and United Methodist churches.[22] The principles which have guided its work and subsequent decisions were enumerated by this writer in a report to the international fellowship of liturgical scholars, *Societas Liturgica*, at its meeting in Paris, France on 25 August 1981 as follows.

1. The basic calendar and structure of three readings presupposed by the Roman Lectionary are assumed.

2. The Gospel pericopes are assumed with only minor textual rearrangement to accommodate churches which use a Bible for liturgical use rather than a Lectionary.

3. The New Testament pericopes are largely accepted with some lengthening of pericopes and minor textual rearrangement to include contextual material such as apostolic and personal greetings and local ecclesial issues.

4. The typological choice of Old Testament pericopes has been addressed in that this has been the area of most serious criticism of the lectionary from Catholic and Protestant scholars and pastors. In response, the Committee has proposed a revision of the Roman table for a number of Sundays of the Year in each of the three cycles. The lessons are still typologically controlled by the Gospel, but in a broader way than Sunday by Sunday, in order to make possible semi-continuous reading of some significant Old Testament narratives.[23]

The report of NACCL for harmonization and adaptation of the Roman Lectionary and its denominational variants is now being recommended to participating churches for trial use, study, and review over the several liturgical years encompassed by 1983-1986. It should be emphasized, in accordance with the principles enunciated above, that this CCT proposal is basically a *harmonization* of existing denominational tables and an *adaptation* of the Old Testament pericopes for the Sundays which follow Pentecost, to accord with a certain broadly-defined typological principle and also to include semi-continuous reading of the Hebrew Bible. In order to describe in fuller detail this CCT proposal it is necessary to identify certain assumptions implicit in the Roman Lectionary (and explicit in its Introduction or *Praenotanda*[24]) and indicate how the CCT table both respects and amplifies those assumptions. They are three in number; they relate to (1) calendar, (2) cult, and (3) canon.

(1) Calendar

Every lectionary makes calendrical assumptions and every calendar carries implications for the lectionary. The intertwined history of calendar and lectionary is well known. Perhaps the most important single assumption of the *annual* calendar which governs the Roman Lectionary is the foundational character of the *weekly* festival of the Lord's Day or Sunday. This is rooted in New Testament language and the earliest traditions of the post-apostolic church. Thus Justin Martyr in his *Apology* (ca. 150 A.D.):

10

It is on Sunday that we all assemble, because Sunday is the first day: the day on which God transformed darkness and matter and created the world, and the day on which Jesus Christ our Savior rose from the dead. He was crucified on the eve of Saturn's day, and on the day after, that is, on the day of the sun, he appeared to his apostles and disciples and taught them what we have now offered for your examination.[25]

Thus also the General Norms for the Liturgical Year and the Calendar as published by the Roman Church in 1969:

The Church celebrates the paschal mystery on the first day of the week, known as the Lord's Day or Sunday. This follows a tradition handed down from the apostles and having its origin from the day of Christ's resurrection. Thus Sunday must be ranked as the first holyday of all.[26]

The weekly Lord's Day as a festival in its own right which celebrates both creation and redemption is expressed in the calendar's designation of 33 or 34 Sundays as *Dominica per annum* ("Sundays in Ordinary Time" or "Sundays of the Year", expressions which unhappily in English do not seem to carry the fullness of the Latin). This weekly festival may be said to be foundational for the entire annual cycle by reason of its Christological focus. Creation was by words ("God said . . .") and through *the* Word (John 1:3) and its first fruit was light (Genesis 1:3 and John 1:4-5). Redemption is in Christ, the light of the world who rose from the dead on the first day of the week.

The church's annual calendar is also Christological in character in that it comprises two great centers separated by intervening Sundays: (a) the Sundays, solemnities and celebrations around Christmas and (b) the Sundays, solemnities and celebrations around Easter. The latter is of course the older of the two and in many ways more formative for the whole calendar. One may say therefore concerning the liturgical celebration of every Sunday, and in particular those Sundays before and after each of the two annual centers:

When in celebrating the liturgy the Church proclaims both the Old and New Testament, it is proclaiming one and the same mystery of Christ. The New Testament lies hidden in the Old; the Old Testament comes fully to light in the New. Christ himself is the center and fullness of all Scripture, as he is of the entire liturgy. Thus the Scriptures are the living waters from which all who seek life and salvation must drink.[27]

Or again (also from the 1981 second edition of the Roman Lectionary):

The liturgy is always the celebration of the mystery of Christ and makes use of the word of God on the basis of its own tradition, guided not by merely logical or extrinsic concerns but by the desire to proclaim the Gospel and to lead those who believe to the fullness of truth.[28]

11

Among the implications of this weekly, Christological cornerstone of the Christian year are the suggestions (more important for many Protestant communities) that that weekly Lord's Day with its lessons must inevitably be marked with the Lord's Supper, and (more important for Roman Catholics) that that weekly Lord's Day with its Mass must inevitably be marked with the homiletical proclamation of the Gospel, though (as the above-quoted paragraph of the second edition points out) without falling into thematic didacticism. For both Catholics and Protestants there is the further caution against the temptation to supplant this Christological focus and cycle with other cycles, commemorations, and denominational observances.[29]

The fact that the annual calendar actually consists of two kinds of Sundays, however, has dictated an important distinction in the way the three lessons of the day relate to one another. Note must be taken of this distinction since it is at this point that the CCT adaptation makes its most serious decision in the direction of revision.

The two "kinds" of Sundays alluded to refer simply to those Sundays on the one hand which form the two Christological centers, Christmas and Easter respectively, and on the other hand, those Sundays (after Epiphany and Pentecost, in "Ordinary Time") which do not.

The Introduction to the 1969 publication of the Roman Lectionary speaks of the two principles of selection in this way:

> Readings for Sundays and holydays have been arranged according to two principles, called the principles of "thematic harmony" and of "semi-continuous reading." The different seasons of the year and the character of each liturgical season determine which principle applies in specific cases.[30]

The 1981 edition says:

> The principles governing the Order of Readings for Sundays and the solemnities of the Lord are called the principles of "harmony" and of "semi-continuous reading." One or the other applies according to the different seasons of the year and the distinctive character of the particular liturgical season.[31]

Thus all three lessons during the seasons of Advent-Christmas-Epiphany (day) and Lent Easter-Pentecost(day) will be found to exhibit "harmonic" or "thematic" unity. But,

> in contrast, the Sundays in Ordinary Time do not have a distinctive character. Thus the texts of both the apostolic and gospel readings are arranged in an order of semi-continuous reading, whereas the Old Testament reading is harmonized with the gospel.[32]

This distinction between the Sundays of the liturgical seasons and those of Ordinary Time has been too little noticed by commentators and homilists who try to force thematic unity on New Testament and gospel passages in Ordinary Time proceeding on separate semi-continuous "tracks." This plan is of some significance too if the issue is which of the first two readings to use on such Sundays.[33]

There are some details in the annual calendar of the Roman Lectionary which have apparently escaped the notice of many who are using it or one of its adaptations. These details have been enforced by the CCT harmonization.

The season of Advent in the Roman calendar is seen very much in relationship to its early placing in some lectionary tables as being not the beginning but the ending of the annual calendar. This is underscored by the similarity in theme between the last Sundays after Pentecost or in Ordinary Time, and the first Sunday in Advent, that theme being eschatological. The second and third Sundays in Advent continue that emphasis as they focus on the ministry and message of John the Baptist. Only the fourth Sunday in Advent explicitly turns to the preparatory events of the incarnation. This sort of Advent will inevitably create pastoral problems due to the universal and powerful cultural anticipation of Christmas during these weeks, and some theological problems for those who have tended to lay little stress on the Return or Second Coming of the Lord.

Following Christmas, the question of the biblical content of Epiphany arises. Even though some liturgical scholarship has advocated a reuniting of birth and baptism themes for Epiphany, the Roman calendar continues the Western tradition of distinguishing them by completing the celebration of the Lord's birth on Epiphany with the Magi narrative and observing the feast of the Lord's Baptism on the Sunday after Epiphany, the First Sunday in Ordinary Time. The danger here for churches not using the Ordinary Time schedule of pericopes is that the baptism lessons occasionally get suppressed by the transfer of the Epiphany lessons to the following Sunday.

The place of widest divergence in the ecumenical use of the Roman Lectionary has been the placing of Transfiguration pericopes (aside from August 6th). The Roman calendar uses the second Sunday in Lent for this purpose, thus balancing the Temptation narratives of the previous Sunday. Only the Presbyterian edition followed this practice. The Episcopal, Lutheran, and United Methodist tables provided these pericopes as a special set for the Last Sunday after Epiphany, reasoning that just as the Sundays after Pentecost are completed with the festival of Christ the King, so should the Sundays after Epiphany have such a climax. Part of the issue here is the question of whether these Sundays are "seasons" or Ordinary Time, and also the character of the Sundays in Lent.

It is the choice of gospel texts for Lent which requires the most extensive reworking of traditional assumptions among Western Christians. Because of the historic assumption that Lent was a time of unrelieved penitence, and also because of the increasing dominance of Holy Week, those Sundays came to be seen as in sequence only with Holy Week and Good Friday. Remembering, however, that the Sundays themselves are not, nor ever have been, fast days, and hence were not and are not counted as part of the Lenten forty days, the Roman Lectionary has reoriented them so that they are in sequence with Easter Day. Further, their ancient significance as the days anticipatory to the baptismal solemnities of the Paschal Vigil has been recovered. The Introduction to the 1969 edition is instructive:

> The gospel selections for the first two Sundays recount the Lord's temptations and transfiguration as recorded in the three Synoptic Gospels.
>
> For Year A on the next three Sundays the gospels are about the Samaritan women, the man born blind, and Lazarus. Since these passages are very important in relation to Christian initiation, they may also be used for Years B and C, especially when there are candidates for baptism. However, for pastoral reasons, many wished another choice of texts for Years B and C and alternative selections have been provided: Year B, texts from John about Christ's future glorification through his cross and resurrection; Year C, texts from Luke on conversion.[34]

And of course, for all the reasons underlying these choices, the older pre-Lent "-gesima" Sundays have been suppressed, as well as the two-week Passiontide. This latter decision effectively conflates (as it would seem to Protestants) what were popularly known respectively as "Passion" and "Palm" Sundays. Whatever the effect of this in Roman circles it might now lead Protestants to recover the Sunday before Easter as a true and full celebration of the Passion rather than the "little Easter" it becomes when the triumphal entry theme takes over the entire service (an interesting instance of the Entry Rite taking over the whole liturgy). And as fewer and fewer of the faithful find it possible to attend public worship during the following week, including Good Friday, this becomes more and more important, pastorally.

These decisions also pave the way for the recovery of the great Easter Triduum in its unity: (1) Holy Thursday Institution of the Supper, with the Footwashing, (2) Good Friday Adoration of the Cross, and (3) the Easter or Paschal Vigil, with its initiatory rites.

Having reoriented the "forty days" of Lent toward the unified Easter Triduum by means of its use of the Sundays in Lent, the Roman calendar has also provided for a new appreciation of the "Great Fifty Days" to Pentecost (literally: the "fiftieth day") with its Sundays, as a continuing paschal celebration. The displacement during this time of an Old Testament pericope has caused some dismay however. This displacement may be explained in a number of ways. In the first instance it may be observed that caution concerning the typological use of the Old Testament would warn against an imposition of resurrection themes on the Hebrew Bible. Secondly, it is a matter of considerable theological import that in addition to those personal witnesses to the resurrection as reported in the four Gospels and 1 Corinthians, the church itself, as described in the book of Acts (which displaces the Old Testament lesson) is the pre-eminent witness. The 1981 second edition of the Roman Lectionary puts this nicely:

> In this Order of Readings, some biblical books are set aside for particular liturgical seasons on the basis of both the intrinsic impor-

tance of subject matter and liturgical tradition. For example, the Western (Ambrosian and Hispanic) and Eastern tradition of reading Acts during the Easter season is respected. This usage results in a clear presentation of how the Church derives the beginning of its entire life from the paschal mystery.[35]

The Introduction to the 1969 edition says of the New Testament selection: The selections from the writings of the apostles are: Year A, First Letter of Peter; Year B, First Letter of John; Year C, Revelation. These texts seem most appropriate to the spirit of the Easter season, a spirit of joyful faith and confident hope.[36]

Pentecost, the festival of the Holy Spirit, brings to conclusion and climax this great progression of seasons and Sundays begun on the First Sunday of Lent with the account of Jesus' being led into the wilderness by the Spirit (Matthew 4:1; Mark 1:12; Luke 4:1-2), and continued with the "forty days" and then the "Great Fifty Days," the Easter Triduum being their turning point. Pentecost too serves well as the conclusion and climax of that other cycle of Christmas-Epiphany wherein by the power of the Holy Spirit (Matthew 1:18, 20; Luke 1:35) the virgin Mary conceived a child who was subsequently manifested to the whole world as Savior and Lord at his baptism by the Spirit in the Jordan (Matthew 3:16; Mark 1:10; Luke 3:22; John 1:32).

(2) Cult

As has been observed already, the documents instituting the Roman Lectionary are quite clear about the liturgical context of the readings contemplated. This context may not be ignored if the rationale for the choice of readings is to be understood. In its simplest terms this means that for Protestant and Anglican communions the eucharistic context must be taken into account since both of these traditions will be using these readings also at non-eucharistic occasions. The Episcopal *Book of Common Prayer* is quite explicit:

> The Psalms and Lessons appointed for the Sundays and for other major Holy Days are intended for use at all public services on such days, except when the same congregation attends two or more services. Thus, the same Lessons are to be read at the principal morning service, whether the Liturgy of the Word takes the form given in the Holy Eucharist, or that of the Daily Office.[37]

This means that many communities will be using these lessons in a context other than that envisioned by the architects of the structure. As the 1981 second edition specifies,

> The Church is nourished spiritually at the table of God's word and at the table of the eucharist; from the one it grows in wisdom and from the other in holiness. In the word of God the divine covenant is announced; in the eucharist the new and everlasting covenant is

renewed. The spoken word of God brings to mind the history of salvation; the eucharist embodies it in the sacramental signs of the liturgy.[38]

This affects the understanding and shape of the homily as well:

Whether the homily explains the biblical word of God proclaimed in the readings or some other text of the liturgy, it must always lead the community of the faithful to celebrate the eucharist wholeheartedly, "so that they may hold fast in their lives to what they have grasped by their faith."[39]

From this living explanation, the word of God proclaimed in the readings and the Church's celebration of the day's liturgy will have greater impact. But this demands that the homily be truly the fruit of meditation, carefully prepared, neither too long nor too short, and suited to all those present, even children and the uneducated.[40]

The latter stipulations of this directive will strike many Protestant and Anglican readers as surprising and provocative in that the non-eucharistic context encourages in their traditions lengthy homilies and assumes the absence of children.

The eucharistic context of this lectionary is clearly also the single most significant factor in the dominance of the Gospel lesson as the "controlling" lesson. Throughout this is the case:

The reading of the gospel is the high point of the liturgy of the word. For this the other readings, in their established sequence from the Old to the New Testament, prepare the assembly.[41]

The proclamation of the gospel always stands as the high point of the liturgy of the word. Thus the liturgical traditions of both the East and the West have consistently continued to preserve some distinction between the books for the readings.[42]

To be sure, there are hermenuetical as well as denominational disputes which revolve around precisely this issue, but it is a liturgical and devotional reality of some seriousness in a number of churches and therefore it is vital to keep its liturgical context clearly in view.

In addition to the context of the liturgy of the word, its structure and components call for our attention. The General Instruction of the Roman Missal may be cited:

Readings from Scripture and the chants between the readings form the main part of the liturgy of the word. The homily, profession of faith, and general intercessions or prayer of the faithful expand and complete this part of the Mass. In the readings, explained by the homily, God is speaking to his people, opening up to them the mystery of redemption and salvation, and nourishing their spirit; Christ is present to the faithful through his own word. Through the chants the people make God's word their own and through the profession of faith affirm their adherence to it. Finally, having been fed by this word, they make their petitions in the general intercessions for the needs of the Church and for the salvation of the whole world.[43]

This provides a liturgy of the word including five components only: (1) readings, (2) chants, (3) homily, (4) profession of faith and (5) general intercessions. Although this rite is considerably richer than many Catholics are used to, especially if all three readings are employed, it is considerably less than that to which many Protestants and Anglicans are used, whose rites often include in this sequence such other actions as offering, greetings, children's occasions, parish notices, and choral performances, as well as congregational hymns. This Roman rite with its sequence is useful in that it reminds the community of the centrality of the readings and homily. For planners of liturgy this is of paramount importance.

As the "chant" component refers to the responsorial psalm and the "Alleluia" before the gospel reading an interesting issue is inevitably raised concerning the language of praise. This is the primacy of the Psalter for sung praise in Christian worship. Once again, Catholics are accustomed to something less and Protestants and Anglicans to something more in this regard. For Catholics the corporate singing of the Psalter, to say nothing of hymns, is a new experience just as for Protestants and Anglicans "hymns of human composure" have all but overwhelmed even the chanted or metrical Psalter. Thus the pre-eminent place of the psalms as praise and prayer is being asserted anew. No one in the contemporary church has better expressed this possibility than Dietrich Bonhoeffer who places the psalms in a Christological, therefore liturgical, context thus:

> If we want to read and to pray the prayers of the Bible and especially the Psalms, therefore, we must not ask first what they have to do with us, but what they have to do with Jesus Christ. We must ask how we can understand the Psalms as God's Word, and then we shall be able to pray them . . . Thus if the Bible also contains a prayerbook, we learn from this that not only that Word which he has to say to us belongs to the Word of God, but also that word which he wants to hear from us, because it is the word of his beloved Son. This is pure grace, that God tells us how we can speak with him and have fellowship with him. We can do it by praying in the name of Jesus Christ. The Psalms are given to us to this end, that we may learn to pray them in the name of Jesus Christ.[44]

The only other aspect of the liturgy of the word which may need some comment is the relationship of the general intercessions to the ministry of the word. The second edition of 1981 describes this relationship in this way:

> Enlightened by God's word and in a sense responding to it, the assembly of the faithful prays in the general intercessions as a rule for the needs of the universal Church and the local community, for

the salvation of the world and those oppressed by any burden, and for special categories of people.[45]

The idea that prayers of intercession are shaped by the readings and homily is, if any thing, stranger to Protestants than Catholics. The further suggestion that the prayers themselves might be offered by some of the faithful[46] is equally revolutionary to both sides. But so to link prayer with proclamation is to recover and re-order much that has been amiss with worship and piety in the Western church.

Another issue which arises in conjunction with the cultic performance of the liturgy of the word and which thus far has admitted of no simple solution is that of biblical translations which are undertaken primarily for their usefulness as public proclamation and which at the same time are respectful of contemporary concerns for language which is expressive, understandable, and non-discriminatory. A number of projects are currently underway in North America which deserve the closest attention of liturgical and musical scholars.

(3) Canon

Inevitably any system for the regular reading of Holy Scripture by the Christian community involves canonical determinations. Ecumenically speaking the most obvious of these is the matter of the use for the first reading of so-called "Apocryphal" or deutero-canonical writings. But more important in the long run must be the Roman Lectionary's "semi-continuous" principle which characterizes more than half of each calendar year. This commitment makes it possible to read virtually the entirety of the Synoptic gospels in a manner that respects their literary structure, and to use the Fourth Gospel in the kind of liturgical context which also respects its inner structure. This same commitment also makes possible the systematic reading of the New Testament's epistles, Book of Acts, and Revelation. At the same time, during the liturgical seasons of Advent-Epiphany and Lent-Pentecost the entire Bible is read through the Christological "spectacles" of the historic faith of the church. As Karl Barth says of scripture as the word of God, "The prophetic apostolic Word is the word, the witness, the proclamation and the preaching of *Jesus Christ*".[47]

The critical and controversial issues concerning the canonical assumptions made by the Roman Lectionary have to do largely with its handling of the Old Testament, which some scholars and liturgists prefer to speak of as the "Hebrew Bible." The criticism takes two forms. In the first instance it is suggested that the invariable practice of choosing the Old Testament lesson to cohere with the gospel is hermenuetically indefensible and limiting:

Congregations are being protected from the insoluble mystery of God by a packaged providence, a packaged morality, even a packaged mystery of Christ. To record the latter view is painful, for the lectionaries show their greatest ingenuity in establishing the correspondence between the two testaments. But while rising to laudable heights, in ways that would have pleased the New Testament writers and the church fathers, they also tend to reduce the Hebrew revelation to a matter of little consequence apart from the fact of Jesus Christ.[48]

This is the other side of the liturgical and Barthian side which affirms Jesus Christ as the center and focus of Christian faith and worship. It also opens up, yet again, the complex issue of the Christian church's relation to Israel: to what extent must the Hebrew scriptures be "christianized" in order to be scripture?! Interestingly enough, the liturgical enterprise may yet have some surprises in store. However far the theological tradition from St. Paul onward has moved away from the religion of the Law, the liturgical tradition has managed to maintain a large measure of that religion's observances, from vigils and hours of prayer to the Christian Passover and Pentecost. It might even be posited that the proper synthesis of Jewish and specifically Christian elements of faith can only be experienced liturgically.

A second criticism of the Roman Lectionary's use of the Old Testament is in a way derivative of the above. This criticism has been particularly vigorous in the Black American churches. It is that because of the typological choice of the first reading it has been impossible to read the Old Testament in a semi-continuous fashion. Thus the great and lengthy narratives of those books have been left to the lectionaries for daily worship, eucharistic and non-eucharistic as in the Daily Office, which for Protestantism are virtually non-existent and which are experienced by the small minority within Catholicism that celebrates the daily office or daily eucharist. This lack in the Sunday lectionary is to a certain extent compensated for in the Easter and Pentecost Vigils of the Roman rite but these too are largely unknown among Protestants. The question which CCT's working group addressed therefore was whether such material might be brought into the Lord's Day eucharistic lectionary. So we turn now to CCT's proposals concerning the Roman-ecumenical lectionary in terms of calendar, cult, and canon, remembering that its principal mandate was to produce a harmonization of the various adaptations of the Roman Lectionary.

(1) Calendar

NACCL was directed by the Consultation to include in its consensus table readings for the following days:

—all Sundays of the (liturgical) year
—Ash Wednesday
—The Easter Triduum, including Easter Sunday evening
—Monday, Tuesday and Wednesday of Holy Week
—the following Christological feasts:
    Christmas (three sets)
    Epiphany
    Ascension

All Saints
Transfiguration
Annunciation
Visitation
Holy Cross
Presentation
Christ the King

—Thanksgiving Day
—New Year's Day (two sets: one as part of the Christological cycle and one as the beginning of the calendar year)[49]

This mandate has been completed. An appropriate psalm or canticle has also been listed for every set of pericope. NACCL did not, however, provide antiphons or refrains since that involved textual and translation questions which it was not in a position to decide. Certain annotations might be helpful, even though it is quite evident that the existing Roman calendar has been taken over in its entirety together with its gospel pericopes.[50]

Advent in the CCT table does not differ from the existing table except for minor changes in versification. Christmas differs only in versification and provides for a Christmas Eve service, a "Shepherds Mass" and the use of John 1. Following Christmas the mystery of the Incarnation is explored with the remaining gospel infancy and childhood narratives, concluding on the Second Sunday after Christmas (when it occurs) with John 1 again. The Epiphany gospel is the story of the Magi and it appears all three years. Three full sets of lessons are given for the Baptism of the Lord (First Sunday after Epiphany). Three full sets are also given for the Last Sunday after Epiphany as Transfiguration.

Ash Wednesday has one set of lessons to be used all three years. Here, as throughout Lent and Easter the only revision is to be found in versification for the sake of harmonization, contextualization, and ease of reading from a Bible rather than from a pointed lectionary, as is the Roman Catholic usage. On the second Sunday of Lent certain options are provided for churches which have read the Transfiguration lessons already. For the Sunday before Easter the option has been provided in the gospel reading for either a Passion reading or an emphasis on the Palms. On Holy Thursday provision is made for either the foot washing narrative or the Last Supper; a rubric is provided directing that the Year A readings are to be used every year if the foot washing emphasis is always required. On Easter Day an Old Testament option is suggested for the first reading for churches which do not keep the Vigil. The same is done on Pentecost. A rubric provides that in such a case the Acts pericope take the place of the second reading. The Easter evening set focuses on the Luke 24 Emmaus appearance of the Lord. Three full sets of readings have been provided for Pentecost and for Trinity Sunday.

One set of pericopes has been provided for the following days: Presentation, Annunciation, Visitation, and Holy Cross. All Saints and Thanksgiving Day have three sets, although the latter are not related to the lectionary's three year system.

(2) Cult

Nothing in the CCT adaptation changes or affects the assumption of a eucharistic context or the structure of the liturgy of the word. The Old Testament material which was brought in after Pentecost (to be described under "Canon") was chosen with the eucharistic context in mind and should, if anything, strengthen the liturgy of the word, especially for children and neophytes in the faith. Of particular delight to the revision committee was the happy way the psalms relate to those Old Testament narratives which they often explicitly celebrate.

(3) Canon

Since it is to be hoped that this adaptation will be enthusiastically accepted by churches and communities which do not receive the Apocrypha as sacred scripture, there has been included a "canonical" alternative at each place such a deutero-canonical pericope appears.

As has already been mentioned, the major revision this CCT adaptation proposes has to do with the first, or Old Testament, reading on the Sundays ("in Ordinary Time") which follow Pentecost and Trinity Sunday. Without abandoning any of the principles of the original Roman scheme, but rather enforcing them, an attempt has been made to respond positively to the theological concern over the too highly stressed typology and the pastoral concern over the lack of semi-continuous, or narrative, reading of the Old Testament. There has also been widespread feeling that the Minor Prophets and the Wisdom literature had been slighted. The way in which this was done was to apply to the first reading on those Sundays the same logic with which the Roman lectionary chose the second and gospel readings:

> the Sundays in Ordinary Time do not have a distinctive character. Thus the texts of both the apostolic and gospel readings are arranged in an order of semi-continuous reading, whereas the Old Testament reading is harmonized with the gospel.[51]

Thus it was determined to use the Sundays following Pentecost for semi-continuous reading of the Old Testament as well and by the choice of books to retain a broad, though not necessarily week-by-week, "harmony" with the gospels. In this way the typological principle was loosened but not abandoned and the semi-continuous principle was reenforced. The following plan was adopted:

Year A (Matthew) — Twenty (20) Sundays of Pentateuchal material (beginning with Abraham's call and concluding with Moses' death)
— Three (3) Sundays of Ruth
— Three (3) Sundays of prophetic eschatological material

Year B (Mark) — Fourteen (14) Sundays of the Davidic narrative (from his anointing to his death)
— Four (4) Sundays of Wisdom literature
— Eight (8) Sundays substantially following the Roman Lectionary

Year C (Luke) — Ten (10) Sundays of the Elijah-Elisha narrative (beginning with Solomon's dedication of the Temple and concluding with Elisha's death)
— Fifteen (15) Sundays of both Major and Minor prophets
— One (1) Sunday from the Roman Lectionary

Although no particular attempt was made to corrolate the Old Testament narrative passages with the gospel lesson week-by-week it was the judgment of the revision committee that to read the pentateuchal material along with Matthew was to respect that gospel's own preoccupation, as also is the case with the pairing of David and Mark, and the prophets and Luke. Where individual Wisdom or prophetic lessons were chosen which were not particularly sequential week-after-week, then "harmony" with the gospel was a criterion of selection.

Old Testament pericopes displaced as a result of this revision have in some cases been placed elsewhere in the lectionary or indexed for their place in the daily eucharistic lectionary of the Roman Church.

Sundays in Ordinary Time have been designated Sundays "after Epiphany" and "Propers" (as in the Episcopal *Book of Common Prayer*). In order to prevent the present unfortunate lack of synchronization between Roman and Episcopal churches on the one hand and some Protestant churches on the other as to which set of lessons is read on what dated Sunday, it has also been decided to label these designated Sundays with actual dates (as in the United Methodist system [52]). Although this may cause some confusion initially it is felt that denominational publishing houses can soon clarify the situation particularly by the use of annual calendars and weekly leaflet series. Readings not needed when the number of Propers (Sundays following Pentecost) is reduced by a late Easter are omitted at the beginning of the post-Pentecost period (as is now the case in Roman, Episcopal, and United Methodist usage). Presbyterians and Lutherans now omit unneeded readings at the end of the liturgical year. The CCT is proposing the first alternative, thereby saving Proper 29 (the last Sunday after Pentecost) for Christ the King. This choice also brings the CCT table into week-to-week conformity with the Roman calendar's designation of the Sundays after Epiphany and the Sundays after Pentecost as Sundays of Ordinary Time.

This harmonization and adaptation of the Roman-ecumenical lectionary is being approved by a number of denominational bodies for trial use and testing. It should be emphasized in conclusion that it is not a large-scale revision of what is now in use so widely and will therefore not displace or render obsolete the many excellent materials now available to clergy, musicians and liturgy planners. It is anticipated that individual denominations will arrange for the gathering of responses during this trial use period.[53] In this way yet a new chapter will be begun in what has been described by one member of the Consultation, Msgr. Frederick McManus, as "by far the most successful and practical ecumenical progress in Christian worship since the Second Vatican Council . . ."[54]

Horace T. Allen, Jr.
Boston, Massachusetts

Footnotes

[1]Sacred Congregation for Divine Worship, *Ordo Lectionum Missae* (Rome: Vatican Polyglot Press, 25 May 1969).

[2]Vatican Council II, Constitution on the Liturgy, *Sacrosanctum Concilium* (4 December 1963; hereafter SC) no. 51, tr. International Commission on English in the Liturgy, *Documents on the Liturgy, 1963-1979: Conciliar, Papal, and Curial Texts* (Collegeville, Minnesota: The Liturgical Press, 1982; hereafter DOL), para. 51.

[3]Sacred Congregation for the Sacraments and Divine Worship, *Lectionary for Mass*, Introduction (Second *Editio Typica*, 1981; hereafter *Lectionary*, 1981) no. 4, tr. International Commission on English in the Liturgy, *Lectionary*, I (London: Collins Liturgical Publications and Cassell Ltd.; Dublin: Veritas Publications; Sydney: E. J. Dwyer Ltd., 1981) and *Liturgy Documentary Series*, 1 (Washington, D.C.: Office of Publishing Services, United States Catholic Conference, 1982).

[4]SC, no. 56, DOL, para. 56.

[5]Coetus XI was one of the working bodies of the post-Vatican II Consilium for the Implementation of the Constitution on the Liturgy.

[6]Gaston Fontaine, C.R.I.C., *"Commentarium ad Ordinem Lectionum Missae,"* *Notitiae*, no. 47 (1969), p. 258, unpublished, tr. International Commission on English in the Liturgy.

[7]The Joint Committee on Worship for Cumberland Presbyterian Church, Presbyterian Church in the United States, and The United Presbyterian Church in the United States of America, *The Worshipbook: Services and Hymns* (Philadelphia: The Westminster Press, 1970).

[8]Standing Liturgical Commission of the Episcopal Church, *Prayer Book Studies 19* (New York, N.Y.: The Church Hymnal Corporation, 1970); Inter-Lutheran Worship Commission, *The Church Year: Contemporary Worship 6* (Minneapolis: Augsburg Publishing House, 1973).

[9]Charles Mortimer Guilbert, Custodian of the Standard Book of Common Prayer of the Protestant Episcopal Church in the United States, *The Draft Proposed Book of Common Prayer and Administration of the Sacraments and Other Rites and Ceremonies of the Church* (New York, N.Y.: The Church Hymnal Corporation, 1976), pp. 888-921.

[10]Charles Mortimer Guilbert, Custodian of the Standard Book of Common Prayer of the Protestant Episcopal Church in the United States, *The Book of Common Prayer and Administration of the Sacraments and Other Rites and Ceremonies of the*

Church (New York, N.Y.: The Church Hymnal Corporation and The Seabury Press, 1979; hereafter *Book of Common Prayer*), pp. 889-921.

[11]Inter-Lutheran Commission on Worship, *Lutheran Book of Worship*, Ministers' Desk Edition (Minneapolis: Augsburg Publishing House; Philadelphia: Board of Publication, Lutheran Church in America, 1978), pp. 121-170.

[12]Section on Worship of the Board of Discipleship of the United Methodist Church, *Word and Table: A Basic Pattern of Sunday Worship for United Methodists* (Nashville: Abingdon Press, 1976), pp. 50-57.

[13]Commission on Worship of the Consultation on Church Union, *A Lectionary* (Princeton: Commission on Worship of the Consultation on Church Union, 1974).

[14]Anglican Church of Canada, *The Lectionary* (Toronto, Ontario: The Anglican Book Center, 1980).

[15]*The Report of the Lambeth Conference 1978* (London: CIO Publishing, 1978), Resolution #24.

[16]Reginald H. Fuller, *Preaching the New Lectionary: The Word of God for the Church Today* (Collegeville, Minnesota: The Liturgical Press, 1974).

[17]Gerard S. Sloyan, *A Commentary on the New Lectionary* (New York, N.Y.: Paulist Press, 1975).

[18]*New Catholic Encyclopedia*, XVII, s.v. "Consultation on Common Texts," by Horace T. Allen, Jr.

[19]"Minutes of the Consultation on Common Texts" (Washington, D.C., 28-31 March 1978).

[20]Ibid.

[21]Lewis A. Briner, Chair, North American Committee on Calendar and Lectionary, "Report to the Consultation on Common Texts," mimeographed (21 November 1980).

[22]Ibid. The Rev. Dr. Lewis A. Briner (Presbyterian), Pastor, Kalamazoo, MI, NACCL Chair; The Rev. Dr. Horace T. Allen, Jr. (Presbyterian), Boston University School of Theology, Boston, MA, Chair, Consultation on Common Texts; Dr. Dianne Bergant, C.S.A. (Roman Catholic), Catholic Theological Union, Chicago, IL; The Rev. Dr. Hans Boehringer (Lutheran Church, Missouri Synod), Pastor, Valparaiso, IN; The Rev. Dr. Richard Eslinger (United Methodist), Board of Discipleship, Nashville, TN; The Rev. Dr. Reginald Fuller (Episcopal), Virginia Theological Seminary, Alexandria, VA; The Rev. Dr. Hoyt Hickman (United Methodist), Board of Discipleship, Nashville, TN; Mr. James M. Schellman (Roman Catholic), International Commission on English in the Liturgy, Washington, D.C., Secretary NACCL; The Rev. Dr. Stanley Schneider (Lutheran), Pastor, Toledo, OH; The Rev. Dr. Carroll Stuhlmueller, C.P. (Roman Catholic), Catholic Theological Union, Chicago, IL.

[23]Horace T. Allen, Jr., "Address to *Societas Liturgica*," mimeographed (Paris: 25 August 1981).

[24]Sacred Congregation for Divine Worship, *Lectionary for Mass*, Introduction (1st ed., 1969; hereafter *Lectionary*, 1969) DOL, paras. 1843-1869.

[25]Lucien Deiss, C.S.Sp., *Springtime of the Liturgy*, (Collegeville, Minnesota: The Liturgical Press, 1979), p. 94.

[26]Sacred Congregation of Rites (Consilium), *General Norms for the Liturgical Year and the Calendar* (21 March 1969; hereafter *General Norms*), no. 4, DOL, para. 3770.

[27]*Lectionary*, 1981, no. 5.

[28]Ibid., no. 68.

[29]*General Norms*, no. 50, DOL, para. 3816.

[30]*Lectionary*, 1969, Ch. I, no. 3, DOL, para. 1845.

[31]*Lectionary*, 1981, no. 66.

[32]Ibid., no. 67.

[33]The *Ordo Lectionum Missae* of 1969 (in no. 318) and the *Ordo* of 1981 (in no. 79) indicated clearly that in liturgical celebrations assigned three readings, all three should be used. Although it is left to conferences of bishops, for pastoral reasons, to permit the use of only two readings in some instances, the conference of Catholic bishops of the United States decided in 1969 to implement fully the revised lectionary with its pattern of three readings on Sundays and feast days. The reasons for this position were: (a) to foster the direction given in no. 51 of the Constitution on the Liturgy, which called for richer fare from Scripture to be set out for the faithful from the table of God's word over a cycle of years; (b) to avoid the likelihood that in allowing a choice of just two readings, this would become the norm in practice. Thus, the thrust of the liturgy constitution would have been frustrated and a preconciliar treatment of Scripture retained.

[34]*Lectionary*, 1969, Ch. II, no. 13, DOL, para. 1856.

[35]*Lectionary*, 1981, no. 74.

[36]*Lectionary*, 1969, Ch. II, no. 14, DOL, para. 1857.

[37]*Book of Common Prayer*, p. 888.

[38]*Lectionary*, 1981, no. 10.

[39]SC, no. 10, DOL, para. 10.

[40]*Lectionary*, 1981, no. 24.

[41]Ibid., no. 13.

[42]Ibid., no. 36.

[43]Sacred Congregation for Divine Worship, *General Instruction of the Roman Missal* (4th ed., 1975), no. 33, DOL, para. 1423.

[44]Dietrich Bonhoeffer, *Psalms: the Prayer Book of the Bible*, tr. James H. Burtness (Minneapolis: Augsburg Publishing House, 1970), pp. 14-15.

[45]*Lectionary*, 1981, no. 30.

[46]Ibid.

[47]Karl Barth, *Church Dogmatics* I/1 *The Doctrine of the Word of God*, tr. G. T. Thomson (Edinburgh: T. & T. Clark, 1936), p. 121.

[48]Gerard S. Sloyan, "The Lectionary as a Context for Interpretation," *Interpretation: A Journal of Bible and Theology*, 31 (April, 1977), p. 138.

[49]Consultation on Common Texts, unpublished minutes, April 1, 1978.

[50]Most of the first readings that appear in the CCT lectionary also appear in the Roman lectionary, together with a specific responsorial psalm containing identified or recommended verses. The Roman lectionary itself is quite flexible in this whole matter. It provides, for example, common or seasonal responsorial psalms.

[51]*Lectionary*, 1981, no. 67.

[52]Section on Worship of the Board of Discipleship of The United Methodist Church, Seasons of the Gospel: Resources for the Christian Year (Nashville: Abingdon Press, 1979).

[53]The International Commission on English in the Liturgy serves as the Secretariat for the Consultation on Common Texts. ICEL's address: 1234 Massachusetts Avenue, N.W., Washington, D.C. 20005, U.S.A.

[54]Frederick R. McManus, "Report on the Consultation on Common Texts to the Episcopal Board of the International Commission on English in the Liturgy" (Washington, D.C.: 6 March 1982).

Table of Readings and Psalms

(Versification follows that of the *Revised Standard Version*)

		First Sunday of Advent	Second Sunday of Advent	Third Sunday of Advent	Fourth Sunday of Advent
A.	Lesson 1	Isaiah 2:1-5 Ps. 122	Isaiah 11:1-10 Ps. 72:1-8	Isaiah 35:1-10 Ps. 146:5-10	Isaiah 7:10-16 Ps. 24
	Lesson 2	Romans 13:11-14	Romans 15:4-13	James 5:7-10	Romans 1:1-7
	Gospel	Matthew 24:36-44	Matthew 3:1-12	Matthew 11:2-11	Matthew 1:18-25
B.	Lesson 1	Isaiah 63:16 - 64:8 Ps. 80:1-7	Isaiah 40:1-11 Ps. 85:8-13	Isaiah 61:1-4,8-11 Luke 1:46b-55	2 Sam 7:8-16 Ps. 89:1-4,19-24
	Lesson 2	1 Cor 1:3-9	2 Peter 3:8-15a	1 Thess 5:16-24	Romans 16:25-27
	Gospel	Mark 13:32-37	Mark 1:1-8	John 1:6-8,19-28	Luke 1:26-38
C.	Lesson 1	Jeremiah 33:14-16 Ps 25:1-10	Baruch 5:1-9 *or* Malachi 3:1-4 Ps 126	Zephaniah 3:14-20 Isaiah 12:2-6	Micah 5:2-5a (5:1-4a) Ps 80:1-7
	Lesson 2	1 Thess 3:9-13	Philip 1:3-11	Philip 4:4-9	Hebrews 10:5-10
	Gospel	Luke 21:25-36	Luke 3:1-6	Luke 3:7-18	Luke 1:39-55

	Christmas, First Proper (Christmas Eve/Day*)	Christmas, Second Proper (Additional Lessons for Christmas Day)	Christmas, Third Proper (Additional Lessons for Christmas Day)
A.			
Lesson 1	Isaiah 9:2-7 Ps 96	Isaiah 62:6-7,10-12 Ps 97	Isaiah 52:7-10 Ps 98
Lesson 2	Titus 2:11-14	Titus 3:4-7	Hebrews 1:1-12
Gospel	Luke 2:1-20	Luke 2:8-20	John 1:1-14

*The readings from the second and third propers for Christmas may be used as alternatives for Christmas day. If the third proper is not used on Christmas day, it should be used at some service during the Christmas cycle because of the significance of John's prologue.

		First Sunday after Christmas*	January 1 - Holy Name of Jesus Solemnity of Mary, Mother of God	January 1 (when observed as New Year)	Second Sunday after Christmas**
A.	Lesson 1	Isaiah 63:7-9 Ps 111	Numbers 6:22-27 Ps 67	Deuteronomy 8:1-10 Ps 117	Jeremiah 31:7-14 or Ecclus 24:1-4,12-16 Ps 147:12-20
	Lesson 2	Hebrews 2:10-18	Galatians 4:4-7 or Philippians 2:9-13	Rev 21:1-6a	Eph 1:3-6,15-18
	Gospel	Matt 2:13-15,19-23	Luke 2:15-21	Matthew 25:31-46	John 1:1-18
B.	Lesson 1	Is 61:10 - 62:3 Ps 111		Eccles 3:1-13 Ps 8	
	Lesson 2	Galatians 4:4-7		Colossians 2:1-7	
	Gospel	Luke 2:22-40		Matthew 9:14-17	
C.	Lesson 1	1 Sam 2:18-20,26 or Ecclus 3:3-7,14-17 Ps 111		Isaiah 49:1-10 Ps 90:1-12	
	Lesson 2	Colossians 3:12-17		Ephesians 3:1-10	
	Gospel	Luke 2:41-52		Luke 14:16-24	

*or the readings for Epiphany.

**or the readings for Epiphany if not otherwise used.

	Epiphany	Baptism of the Lord (1st Sunday after Epiphany)*	2nd Sunday after Epiphany	3rd Sunday after Epiphany	4th Sunday after Epiphany
A.					
Lesson 1	Isaiah 60:1-6 Ps 72:1-14	Isaiah 42:1-9 Ps 29	Isaiah 49:1-7 Ps 40:1-11	Isaiah 9:1-4 Ps 27:1-6	Micah 6:1-8 Ps 37:1-11
Lesson 2	Ephesians 3:1-12	Acts 10:34-43	1 Cor 1:1-9	1 Cor 1:10-17	1 Cor 1:18-31
Gospel	Matthew 2:1-12	Matthew 3:13-17	John 1:29-34	Matthew 4:12-23	Matthew 5:1-12
B.					
Lesson 1		Genesis 1:1-5 Ps 29	1 Sam 3:1-10,(11-20) Ps 63:1-8	Jonah 3:1-5,10 Ps 62:5-12	Deut 18:15-20 Ps 111
Lesson 2		Acts 19:1-7	1 Cor 6:12-20	1 Cor 7:29-31 (32-35)	1 Cor 8:1-13
Gospel		Mark 1:4-11	John 1:35-42	Mark 1:14-20	Mark 1:21-28
C.					
Lesson 1		Isaiah 61:1-4 Ps 29	Isaiah 62:1-5 Ps 36:5-10	Neh 8:1-4a,5-6,8-10 Ps 19:7-14	Jeremiah 1:4-10 Ps 71:1-6
Lesson 2		Acts 8:14-17	1 Cor 12:1-11	1 Cor 12:12-30	1 Cor 13:1-13
Gospel		Luke 3:15-17,21-22	John 2:1-11	Luke 4:14-21	Luke 4:21-30

*In Leap Years, the number of Sundays after Epiphany will be the same as if Easter Day were one day later.

	5th Sunday after Epiphany	6th Sunday after Epiphany (Proper 1)	7th Sunday after Epiphany (Proper 2)	8th Sunday after Epiphany (Proper 3)	Last Sunday after Epiphany Transfiguration
A. Lesson 1	Isaiah 58:3-9a Ps 112:4-9	Deut 30:15-20 or Ecclus 15:15-20 Ps 119:1-8	Isaiah 49:8-13 Ps 62:5-12	Lev 19:1-2,9-18 Ps 119:33-40	Exodus 24:12-18 Ps 2:6-11
Lesson 2	1 Cor 2:1-11	1 Cor 3:1-9	1 Cor 3:10-11,16-23	1 Cor 4:1-5	2 Peter 1:16-21
Gospel	Matthew 5:13-16	Matthew 5:17-26	Matthew 5:27-37	Matthew 5:38-48	Matthew 17:1-9
B. Lesson 1	Job 7:1-7 Ps 147:1-11	2 Kings 5:1-14 Ps 32	Isaiah 43:18-25 Ps 41	Hosea 2:14-20 Ps 103:1-13	2 Kings 2:1-12a Ps 50:1-6
Lesson 2	1 Cor 9:16-23	1 Cor 9:24-27	2 Cor 1:18-22	2 Cor 3:1-6	2 Cor 4:3-6
Gospel	Mark 1:29-39	Mark 1:40-45	Mark 2:1-12	Mark 2:18-22	Mark 9:2-9
C. Lesson 1	Isaiah 6:1-8(9-13) Ps 138	Jeremiah 17:5-10 Ps 1	Genesis 45:3-11,15 Ps 37:1-11	Ecclus 27:4-7 or Isaiah 55:10-13 Ps 92:1-4,12-15	Exodus 34:29-35 Ps 99
Lesson 2	1 Cor 15:1-11	1 Cor 15:12-20	1 Cor 15:35-38 42-50	1 Cor 15:51-58	2 Cor 3:12 - 4:2
Gospel	Luke 5:1-11	Luke 6:17-26	Luke 6:27-38	Luke 6:39-49	Luke 9:28-36

	Ash Wednesday	First Sunday of Lent	Second Sunday of Lent	Third Sunday of Lent	Fourth Sunday of Lent
A. Lesson 1	Joel 2:1-2,12-17a Ps 51:1-12	Genesis 2:4b-9, 15-17,25 - 3:7 Ps 130	Genesis 12:1-4a (4b-8) Ps 33:18-22	Exodus 17:3-7 Ps 95	1 Sam 16:1-13 Ps 23
Lesson 2	2 Cor 5:20b - 6:2 (3-10)	Romans 5:12-19	Romans 4:1-5, (6-12),13-17	Romans 5:1-11	Ephesians 5:8-14
Gospel	Matthew 6:1-6,16-21	Matthew 4:1-11	John 3:1-17 *or* Matthew 17:1-9	John 4:5-26 (27-42)	John 9:1-41
B. Lesson 1		Genesis 9:8-17 Ps 25:1-10	Genesis 17:1-10, 15-19 Ps 105:1-11	Exodus 20:1-17 Ps 19:7-14	2 Chron 36:14-23 Ps 137:1-6
Lesson 2		1 Peter 3:18-22	Romans 4:16-25	1 Cor 1:22-25	Ephesians 2:4-10
Gospel		Mark 1:9-15	Mark 8:31-38 *or* Mark 9:1-9	John 2:13-22	John 3:14-21
C. Lesson 1		Deuteronomy 26:1-11 Ps 91:9-16	Genesis 15:1-12, 17-18 Ps 127	Exodus 3:1-15 Ps 103:1-13	Joshua 5:9-12 Ps 34:1-8
Lesson 2		Romans 10:8b-13	Philip 3:17 - 4:1	1 Cor 10:1-13	2 Cor 5:16-21
Gospel		Luke 4:1-13	Luke 13:31-35 *or* Luke 9:28-36	Luke 13:1-9	Luke 15:1-3,11-32

		Fifth Sunday of Lent	Lent 6 when observed as Passion Sunday	Lent 6 when observed as Palm Sunday*
A.	Lesson 1	Ezekiel 37:1-14 Ps 116:1-9	Isaiah 50:4-9a Ps 31:9-16	Isaiah 50:4-9a Ps 118:19-29
	Lesson 2	Romans 8:6-11	Philippians 2:5-11	Philippians 2:5-11
	Gospel	John 11:(1-16), 17-45	Matt 26:14 - 27:66 *or* Matt 27:11-54	Matthew 21:1-11
B.	Lesson 1	Jeremiah 31:31-34 Ps 51:10-17	Same as A Ps 31:9-16	Same as A Ps 118:19-29
	Lesson 2	Hebrews 5:7-10	Same as A	Same as A
	Gospel	John 12:20-33	Mark 14:1 - 15:47 *or* Mark 15:1-39	Mark 11:1-11 *or* John 12:12-16
C.	Lesson 1	Isaiah 43:16-21 Ps 126	Same as A Ps 31:9-16	Same as A Ps 118:19-29
	Lesson 2	Philippians 3:8-14	Same as A	Same as A
	Gospel	John 12:1-8	Luke 22:14 - 23:56 *or* Luke 23:1-49	Luke 19:28-40

*These readings are provided for the liturgy or procession of palms for also for an early "said" service in the Episcopal tradition. Churches which have not had the tradition of readings-and-procession and

Holy Week

		Monday	Tuesday	Wednesday	Holy Thursday***	Good Friday
A.	Lesson 1	Isaiah 42:1-9 Ps 36:5-10	Isaiah 49:1-7 Ps 71:1-12	Isaiah 50:4-9a Ps 70	Exodus 12:1-14 Ps 116:12-19	Isaiah 52:13 - 53:12 Ps 22:1-18
	Lesson 2	Hebrews 9:11-15	1 Cor 1:18-31	Hebrews 12:1-3	1 Cor 11:23-26	Hebrews 4:14-16, 5:7-9
	Gospel	John 12:1-11	John 12:20-36	John 13:21-30	John 13:1-15	John 18:1 - 19:42 *or* John 19:17-30
B.	Lesson 1				Exodus 24:3-8 Ps 116:12-19	
	Lesson 2				1 Cor 10:16-17	
	Gospel				Mark 14:12-26	
C.	Lesson 1				Jeremiah 31:31-34 Ps 116:12-19	
	Lesson 2				Hebrews 10:16-25	
	Gospel				Luke 22:7-20	

*for those who want the feet washing emphasis every year, "A" readings are used each year.

**Psalm 116 is used at the Lord's Supper on Holy Thursday. Psalm 89:20-21,24,26 is used at the "chrism" service.

Easter Vigil*

Old Testament Readings and Psalms (A, B, C)

Genesis 1:1 - 2:2
    Psalm 33

Genesis 7:1-5,11-18;8:6-18;9:8-13
    Psalm 46

Genesis 22:1-18
    Psalm 16

Exodus 14:10 - 15:1
    Exodus 15:1-6,11-13,17-18

Isaiah 54:5-14
    Psalm 30

Isaiah 55:1-11
    Isaiah 12:2-6

Baruch 3:9-15,32 - 4:4
    Psalm 19

Ezekiel 36:24-28
    Psalm 42

Ezekiel 37:1-14
    Psalm 143

Zephaniah 3:14-20
    Psalm 98

Second Reading (A, B, C)

Romans 6:3-11
    Psalm 114

Gospel

A. Matthew 28:1-10
B. Mark 16:1-8
C. Luke 24:1-12

*This selection of readings and psalms is provided for the Easter Vigil. A minimum of three readings from the Old Testament should be used, and this should always include Exodus 14.

		Easter***	Second Sunday of Easter	Third Sunday of Easter	Fourth Sunday of Easter	Fifth Sunday of Easter
A.	Lesson 1	Acts 10:34-43 *or* Jeremiah 31:1-6 Ps 118:14-24	Acts 2:14a,22-32 Ps 16:5-11	Acts 2:14a,36-41 Ps 116:12-19	Acts 2:42-47 Ps 23	Acts 7:55-60 Ps 31:1-8
	Lesson 2	Colossians 3:1-4 *or* Acts 10:34-43	1 Peter 1:3-9	1 Peter 1:17-23	1 Peter 2:19-25	1 Peter 2:2-10
	Gospel	John 20:1-18 *or* Matthew 28:1-10	John 20:19-31	Luke 24:13-35	John 10:1-10	John 14:1-14
B.	Lesson 1	Acts 10:34-43 *or* Isaiah 25:6-9 Ps 118:14-24	Acts 4:32-35 Ps 133	Acts 3:12-19 Ps 4	Acts 4:8-12 Ps 23	Acts 8:26-40 Ps 22:25-31
	Lesson 2	1 Cor 15:1-11 *or* Acts 10:34-43	1 John 1:1 - 2:2	1 John 3:1-7	1 John 3:18-24	1 John 4:7-12
	Gospel	John 20:1-18 *or* Mark 16:1-8	John 20:19-31	Luke 24:35-48	John 10:11-18	John 15:1-8

Continued on page 38

Continued from page 37

		Easter***	Second Sunday of Easter	Third Sunday of Easter	Fourth Sunday of Easter	Fifth Sunday of Easter
C.	Lesson 1	Acts 10:34-43 _or_ Isaiah 65:17-25 Ps 118:14-24	Acts 5:27-32 Ps 2	Acts 9:1-20 Ps 30:4-12	Acts 13:15-16,26-33 Ps 23	Acts 14:8-18 Ps 145:13b-21
	Lesson 2	1 Cor 15:19-26 _or_ Acts 10:34-43	Revelation 1:4-8	Revelation 5:11-14	Revelation 7:9-17	Revelation 21:1-6
	Gospel	John 20:1-18 _or_ Luke 24:1-12	John 20:19-31	John 21:1-19 _or_ John 21:15-19	John 10:22-30	John 13:31-35

*See next page for Easter Evening.

**If the Old Testament passage is chosen for the first reading, the Acts passage is used as the second reading in order to initiate the sequential reading of Acts during the fifty days of Easter.

Easter Evening*

A.	Lesson 1	Acts 5:29-32 _or_ Daniel 12:1-3 Ps 150
	Lesson 2	1 Cor 5:6-8 _or_ Acts 5:29-32
	Gospel	Luke 24:13-49

*If the first reading is from the Old Testament, the reading from Acts should be second.

38

	Sixth Sunday of Easter	Ascension*	Seventh Sunday Easter	Pentecost**	Trinity Sunday
A. **Lesson 1**	Acts 17:22-31 Ps 66:8-20	Acts 1:1-11 Ps 47	Acts 1:6-14 Ps 68:1-10	Acts 2:1-21 *or* Isaiah 44:1-8 Ps 104:24-34	Deuteronomy 4:32-40 Ps 33:1-12
Lesson 2	1 Peter 3:13-22	Ephesians 1:15-23	1 Peter 4:12-14; 5:6-11	1 Cor 12:3b-13 *or* Acts 2:1-21	2 Cor 13:5-14
Gospel	John 14:15-21	Luke 24:46-53 *or* Mark 16:9-16,19-20	John 17:1-11	John 20:19-23 *or* John 7:37-39	Matthew 28:16-20
B. **Lesson 1**	Acts 10:44-48 Ps 98	Ps 47	Acts 1:15-17,21-26 Ps 1	Acts 2:1-21 *or* Ezekiel 37:1-14 Ps 104:24-34	Isaiah 6:1-8 Ps 29
Lesson 2	1 John 5:1-6		1 John 5:9-13	Romans 8:22-27 *or* Acts 2:1-21	Romans 8:12-17
Gospel	John 15:9-17		John 17:11b-19	John 15:26-27; 16:4b-15	John 3:1-17

Continued on page 40

Continued from page 39

	Sixth Sunday of Easter	Ascension*	Seventh Sunday Easter	Pentecost**	Trinity Sunday
C. Lesson 1	Acts 15:1-2,22-29 Ps 67	Ps 47	Acts 16:16-34 Ps 97	Acts 2:1-21 *or* Genesis 11:1-9 Ps 104:24-34	Proverbs 8:22-31 Ps 8
Lesson 2	Rev 21:10,22-27		Rev 22:12-14,16-17,20	Romans 8:14-17 *or* Acts 2:1-21	Romans 5:1-5
Gospel	John 14:23-29		John 17:20-26	John 14:8-17,25-27	John 16:12-15

*or on Seventh Sunday of Easter.

**If the Old Testament passage is chosen for the first reading, the Acts passage is used as the second reading.

		Proper 4* Sunday between May 29 and June 4 inclusive (If after Trinity Sunday)	Proper 5 Sunday between June 5 and 11 inclusive (If after Trinity Sunday)	Proper 6 Sunday between June 12 and 18 inclusive (If after Trinity Sunday)	Proper 7 Sunday between June 19 and 25 inclusive (If after Trinity Sunday)	Proper 8 Sunday between June 26 and July 2 inclusive
A.	Lesson 1	Genesis 12:1-9 Ps 33:12-22	Genesis 22:1-18 Ps 13	Genesis 25:19-34 Ps 46	Genesis 28:10-17 Ps 91:1-10	Genesis 32:22-32 Ps 17:1-7,15
	Lesson 2	Romans 3:21-28	Romans 4:13-18	Romans 5:6-11	Romans 5:12-19	Romans 6:3-11
	Gospel	Matthew 7:21-29	Matthew 9:9-13	Matt 9:35 - 10:8	Matthew 10:24-33	Matthew 10:34-42
B.	Lesson 1	1 Sam 16:1-13 Ps 20	1 Sam 16:14-23 Ps 57	2 Sam 1:1,17-27 Ps 46	2 Sam 5:1-12 Ps 48	2 Sam 6:1-15 Ps 24
	Lesson 2	2 Cor 4:5-12	2 Cor 4:13 - 5:1	2 Cor 5:6-10,14-17	2 Cor 5:18 - 6:2	2 Cor 8:7-15
	Gospel	Mark 2:23 - 3:6	Mark 3:20-35	Mark 4:26-34	Mark 4:35-41	Mark 5:21-43
C.	Lesson 1	1 Kings 8:22-23, 41-43 Ps 100	1 Kings 17:17-24 Ps 113	1 Kings 19:1-8 Ps 42	1 Kings 19:9-14 Ps 43	1 Kings 19:15-21 Ps 44:1-8
	Lesson 2	Galatians 1:1-10	Galatians 1:11-24	Galatians 2:15-21	Galatians 3:23-29	Galatians 5:1,13-25
	Gospel	Luke 7:1-10	Luke 7:11-17	Luke 7:36 - 8:3	Luke 9:18-24	Luke 9:51-62

*If the Sunday between May 24 and 28 inclusive follows Trinity Sunday, use Eighth Sunday after Epiphany on that day.

		Proper 9 Sunday between July 3 and 9 inclusive	Proper 10 Sunday between July 10 and 16 inclusive	Proper 11 Sunday between July 17 and 23 inclusive	Proper 12 Sunday between July 24 and 30 inclusive	Proper 13 Sunday between July 31 and Aug. 6 inclusive
A.	Lesson 1	Exodus 1:6-14,22 -2:10 / Ps 124	Exodus 2:11-22 / Ps 69:6-15	Exodus 3:1-12 / Ps 103:1-13	Exodus 3:13-20 / Ps 105:1-11	Exodus 12:1-14 / Ps 143:1-10
	Lesson 2	Romans 7:14-25a	Romans 8:9-17	Romans 8:18-25	Romans 8:26-30	Romans 8:31-39
	Gospel	Matthew 11:25-30	Matt 13:1-9,18-23	Matt 13:24-30,36-43	Matthew 13:44-52	Matthew 14:13-21
B.	Lesson 1	2 Samuel 7:1-17 / Ps 89:20-37	2 Samuel 7:18-29 / Ps 132:11-18	2 Samuel 11:1-15 / Ps 53	2 Samuel 12:1-14 / Ps 32	2 Samuel 12:15b-24 / Ps 34:11-22
	Lesson 2	2 Cor 12:1-10	Ephesians 1:1-10	Ephesians 2:11-22	Ephesians 3:14-21	Ephesians 4:1-6
	Gospel	Mark 6:1-6	Mark 6:7-13	Mark 6:30-34	John 6:1-15	John 6:24-35
C.	Lesson 1	1 Kings 21:1-3, 17-21 / Ps 5:1-8	2 Kings 2:1,6-14 / Ps 139:1-12	2 Kings 4:8-17 / Ps 139:13-18	2 Kings 5:1-15ab ("...in Israel") / Ps 21:1-7	2 Kings 13:14-20a / Ps 28
	Lesson 2	Galatians 6:7-18	Colossians 1:1-14	Colossians 1:21-29	Colossians 2:6-15	Colossians 3:1-11
	Gospel	Luke 10:1-12,17-20	Luke 10:25-37	Luke 10:38-42	Luke 11:1-13	Luke 12:13-21

		Proper 14 Sunday between August 7 and 13 inclusive	Proper 15 Sunday between August 14 and 20 inclusive	Proper 16 Sunday between August 21 and 27 inclusive	Proper 17 Sunday between August 28 and Sept. 3 inclusive	Proper 18 Sunday between Sept. 4 and 10 inclusive
A.	Lesson 1	Exodus 14:19-31 Ps 106:4-12	Exodus 16:2-15 Ps 78:1-3,10-20	Exodus 17:1-7 Ps 95	Exodus 19:1-9 Ps 114	Exodus 19:16-24 Ps 115:1-11
	Lesson 2	Romans 9:1-5	Romans 11:13-16, 29-32	Romans 11:33-36	Romans 12:1-13	Romans 13:1-10
	Gospel	Matthew 14:22-33	Matthew 15:21-28	Matthew 16:13-20	Matthew 16:21-28	Matthew 18:15-20
B.	Lesson 1	2 Sam 18:1,5,9-15 Ps 143:1-8	2 Sam 18:24-33 Ps 102:1-12	2 Samuel 23:1-7 Ps 67	1 Kings 2:1-4,10-12 Ps 121	Ecclus 5:8-15 or Proverbs 2:1-8 Ps 119:129-136
	Lesson 2	Eph 4:25 - 5:2	Ephesians 5:15-20	Ephesians 5:21-33	Ephesians 6:10-20	James 1:17-27
	Gospel	John 6:35,41-51	John 6:51-58	John 6:55-69	Mark 7:1-8,14-15, 21-23	Mark 7:31-37
C.	Lesson 1	Jeremiah 18:1-11 Ps 14	Jeremiah 20:7-13 Ps 10:12-18	Jeremiah 28:1-9 Ps 84	Ezekiel 18:1-9,25-29 Ps 15	Ezekiel 33:1-11 Ps 94:12-22
	Lesson 2	Hebrews 11:1-3, 8-19	Heb 12:1-2,12-17	Hebrews 12:18-29	Hebrews 13:1-8	Philemon 1-20
	Gospel	Luke 12:32-40	Luke 12:49-56	Luke 13:22-30	Luke 14:1,7-14	Luke 14:25-33

		Proper 19 Sunday between Sept. 11 and 17 inclusive	Proper 20 Sunday between Sept. 18 and 24 inclusive	Proper 21 Sunday between Sept. 25 and Oct. 1 inclusive	Proper 22 Sunday between Oct. 2 and 8 inclusive	Proper 23 Sunday between Oct. 9 and 15 inclusive
A.	Lesson 1	Exodus 20:1-20 Ps 19:7-14	Exodus 32:1-14 Ps 106:7-8,19-23	Exodus 33:12-23 Ps 99	Numbers 27:12-23 Ps 81:1-10	Deuteronomy 34:1-12 Ps 135:1-14
	Lesson 2	Romans 14:5-12	Philippians 1:21-27	Philippians 2:1-13	Philippians 3:12-21	Philippians 4:1-9
	Gospel	Matthew 18:21-35	Matthew 20:1-16	Matthew 21:28-32	Matthew 21:33-43	Matthew 22:1-14
B.	Lesson 1	Proverbs 22:1-2,8-9 Ps 125	Job 28:20-28 Ps 27:1-6	Job 42:1-6 Ps 27:7-14	Genesis 2:18-24 Ps 128	Genesis 3:8-19 Ps 90:1-12
	Lesson 2	James 2:1-5,8-10, 14-17	James 3:13-18	James 4:13-17, 5:7-11	Heb 1:1-4,2:9-11	Heb 4:1-3,9-13
	Gospel	Mark 8:27-38	Mark 9:30-37	Mark 9:38-50	Mark 10:2-16	Mark 10:17-30
C.	Lesson 1	Hosea 4:1-3,5:15-6:6 Ps 77:11-20	Hosea 11:1-11 Ps 107:1-9	Joel 2:23-30 Ps 107:1,33-43	Amos 5:6-7,10-15 Ps 101	Micah 1:2;2:1-10 Ps 26
	Lesson 2	1 Timothy 1:12-17	1 Timothy 2:1-7	1 Timothy 6:6-19	2 Timothy 1:1-14	2 Timothy 2:8-15
	Gospel	Luke 15:1-10	Luke 16:1-13	Luke 16:19-31	Luke 17:5-10	Luke 17:11-19

		Proper 24 Sunday between October 16 and 22 inclusive	Proper 25 Sunday between October 23 and 29 inclusive	Proper 26 Sunday between October 30 and Nov. 5 inclusive	Proper 27 Sunday between November 6 and 12 inclusive	Proper 28 Sunday between November 13 and 19 inclusive
A.	Lesson 1	Ruth 1:1-19a Ps 146	Ruth 2:1-13 Ps 128	Ruth 4:7-17 Ps 127	Amos 5:18-24 Ps 50:7-15	Zephaniah 1:7,12-18 Ps 76
	Lesson 2	1 Thess 1:1-10	1 Thess 2:1-8	1 Thess 2:9-13,17-20	1 Thess 4:13-18	1 Thess 5:1-11
	Gospel	Matthew 22:15-22	Matthew 22:34-46	Matthew 23:1-12	Matthew 25:1-13	Matthew 25:14-30
B.	Lesson 1	Isaiah 53:7-12 Ps 35:17-28	Jeremiah 31:7-9 Ps 126	Deuteronomy 6:1-9 Ps 119:33-48	1 Kings 17:8-16 Ps 146	Daniel 7:9-14 Ps 145:8-13
	Lesson 2	Hebrews 4:14-16	Hebrews 5:1-6	Hebrews 7:23-28	Hebrews 9:24-28	Hebrews 10:11-18
	Gospel	Mark 10:35-45	Mark 10:46-52	Mark 12:28-34	Mark 12:38-44	Mark 13:24-32
C.	Lesson 1	Habakkuk 1:1-3, 2:1-4 Ps 119:137-144	Zephaniah 3:1-9 Ps 3	Haggai 2:1-9 Ps 65:1-8	Zechariah 7:1-10 Ps 9:11-20	Malachi 4:1-6 (3:19-24 in Heb) Ps 82
	Lesson 2	2 Tim 3:14 - 4:5	2 Tim 4:6-8,16-18	2 Thess 1:5-12	2 Thess 2:13 - 3:5	2 Thess 3:6-13
	Gospel	Luke 18:1-8	Luke 18:9-14	Luke 19:1-10	Luke 20:27-38	Luke 21:5-19

**Proper 29
(Christ the King)
Sunday between
Nov. 20 and 26
inclusive**

A.	Lesson 1	Ezekiel 34:11-16,20-24
		Ps 23
	Lesson 2	1 Cor 15:20-28
	Gospel	Matthew 25:31-46
B.	Lesson 1	Jeremiah 23:1-6
		Ps 93
	Lesson 2	Revelation 1:4b-8
	Gospel	John 18:33-37
C.	Lesson 1	2 Samuel 5:1-5
		Ps 95
	Lesson 2	Colossians 1:11-20
	Gospel	John 12:9-19

A.

	Annunciation March 25	Visitation May 31	Presentation February 2	Holy Cross September 14
Lesson 1	Isaiah 7:10-14 Ps 45 or 40:6-10	1 Samuel 2:1-10 Ps 113	Malachi 3:1-4 Ps 84 or 24:7-10	Numbers 21:4b-9 Ps 98:1-5 or Ps 78:1-2,34-38
Lesson 2	Hebrews 10:4-10	Romans 12:9-16b	Hebrews 2:14-18	1 Cor 1:18-24
Gospel	Luke 1:26-38	Luke 1:39-57	Luke 2:22-40	John 3:13-17

		All Saints, November 1*	Thanksgiving Day**
A.	Lesson 1	Revelation 7:9-17 Ps 34:1-10	Deuteronomy 8:7-18 Ps 65
	Lesson 2	1 John 3:1-3	2 Cor 9:6-15
	Gospel	Matthew 5:1-12	Luke 17:11-19
B.	Lesson 1	Revelation 21:1-6a Ps 24:1-6	Joel 2:21-27 Ps 126
	Lesson 2	Colossians 1:9-14	1 Timothy 2:1-7
	Gospel	John 11:32-44	Matthew 6:25-33
C.	Lesson 1	Daniel 7:1-3,15-18 Ps 149	Deuteronomy 26:1-11 Ps 100
	Lesson 2	Ephesians 1:11-23	Philippians 4:4-9
	Gospel	Luke 6:20-36	John 6:25-35

*or on first Sunday in November.

**readings *ad libitum*, not tied to A, B, or C.

Titles of Seasons, Sundays, and Special Days

Advent Season

First Sunday of Advent . . . . The Sunday occurring November 27 to December 3

Second Sunday of Advent. . . . . The Sunday occurring December 4 to December 10.

Third Sunday of Advent . . . . The Sunday occurring December11 to December 17

Fourth Sunday of Advent . . . . The Sunday occurring December 18 to December 24.

Christmas Season

Christmas Eve/Day . . . . December 24/25.

First Sunday After Christmas. The Sunday occurring December 26 to January 1.

New Year's Eve/Day . . . . December 31 to January 1.

Second Sunday after Christmas . . . . The Sunday occurring January 2 to January 5.

Epiphany Season

Epiphany . . . . January 6 or first Sunday in January.

First Sunday after Epiphany (Baptism of the Lord) . . . . The Sunday occurring January 7 to January 13.

Second Sunday after Epiphany . . . . The Sunday occurring January 14 to January 20.

Third Sunday after Epiphany . . . . The Sunday occurring January 21 to January 27.

Fourth Sunday after Epiphany* . . . . The Sunday occurring January 28 to February 3.

Fifth Sunday after Epiphany* . . . . The Sunday occurring February 4 to February 10.

Sixth Sunday after Epiphany (Proper 1)* . . . . The Sunday occurring February 11 to February 17.

Seventh Sunday after Epiphany (Proper 2)* . . . . The Sunday occurring February 18 to February 24.

Eighth Sunday after Epiphany (Proper 3)* . . . . The Sunday occurring February 25 to February 29.

Last Sunday after Epiphany (Transfiguration Sunday)

*except when this Sunday is the Last Sunday after Epiphany.

Lenten Season

Ash Wednesday: Seventh Wednesday Before Easter
First Sunday of Lent
Second Sunday of Lent
Third Sunday of Lent
Fourth Sunday of Lent
Fifth Sunday of Lent

Holy Week

Passion/Palm Sunday
Monday in Holy Week
Tuesday in Holy Week
Wednesday in Holy Week
Holy Thursday
Good Friday
(Holy Saturday)

Easter Season

Easter Vigil
Easter
Easter Evening
Second Sunday of Easter
Third Sunday of Easter
Fourth Sunday of Easter
Fifth Sunday of Easter
Sixth Sunday of Easter
Ascension (fortieth day, sixth Thursday of Easter)
Seventh Sunday of Easter
Pentecost

Season After Pentecost

Trinity Sunday (First Sunday after Pentecost)
Propers 4-28 (See NOTE below.)
Proper 29, Christ the King: the Sunday occurring November 20 to 26.

Special Days

Some special days observed by many churches are included in the table, with appropriate readings and psalms.

NOTE: Easter is a moveable feast, and can occur as early as March 22 and as late as April 25. When Easter is early, it encroaches on the Sundays after Epiphany, reducing their number, as necessary, from as many as nine to as few as four. In similar fashion the date of Easter determines the number of Sunday Propers after Pentecost. When Easter is as early as March 22, the numbered Proper for the Sunday following Trinity Sunday is Proper 3.

Comparative List of Titles
for Sundays and Special Days

First Sunday of/in Advent

Second Sunday of/in Advent

Third Sunday of/in Advent

Fourth Sunday of/in Advent

Christmas, First Proper/Mass at Midnight/Christmas Day 1

Christmas, Second Proper/Mass at Dawn/Christmas Day II

Christmas, Third Proper/Mass during the day/Christmas Day III

First Sunday after Christmas/Sunday in the Octave of Christmas

January 1/Solemnity of Mary, Mother of God/Holy Name/New Year

Second Sunday after Christmas

Epiphany

Baptism of the Lord/First Sunday after Epiphany

Second Sunday after Epiphany/Second Sunday in Ordinary Time

Third Sunday after Epiphany/Third Sunday in Ordinary Time

Fourth Sunday after Epiphany/Fourth Sunday in Ordinary Time

Fifth Sunday after Epiphany/Fifth Sunday in Ordinary Time

Sixth Sunday after Epiphany/Sixth Sunday in Ordinary Time

Seventh Sunday after Epiphany/Seventh Sunday in Ordinary Time

Eighth Sunday after Epiphany/Eighth Sunday in Ordinary Time

Last Sunday after Epiphany/Transfiguration

Ash Wednesday	Fourth Sunday of/in Lent
First Sunday of/in Lent	Fifth Sunday of/in Lent
Second Sunday of/in Lent	Passion/Palm Sunday
Third Sunday of/in Lent	Monday in Holy Week

Tuesday in Holy Week

Wednesday in Holy Week

Holy/Maundy Thursday

Good Friday

Easter Vigil

Easter

Easter Evening

Second Sunday of Easter

Third Sunday of Easter

Fourth Sunday of Easter

Fifth Sunday of Easter

Sixth Sunday of Easter

Ascension

Seventh Sunday of Easter

Pentecost

Trinity Sunday/First Sunday after Pentecost

Proper 4 (Sunday between May 29 and June 4 inclusive)/Ninth Sunday in Ordinary Time

Proper 5 (Sunday between June 5 and 11 inclusive)/Tenth Sunday in Ordinary Time

Proper 6 (Sunday between June 12 and 18 inclusive)/Eleventh Sunday in Ordinary Time

Proper 7 (Sunday between June 19 and 25 inclusive)/Twelfth Sunday in Ordinary Time

Proper 8 (Sunday between June 26 and July 2 inclusive)/Thirteenth Sunday in Ordinary Time

Proper 9 (Sunday between July 3 and 9 inclusive)/Fourteenth Sunday in Ordinary Time

Proper 10 (Sunday between July 10 and 16 inclusive)/Fifteenth Sunday in Ordinary Time

Proper 11 (Sunday between July 17 and 23 inclusive)/Sixteenth Sunday in Ordinary Time

Proper 12 (Sunday between July 24 and 30 inclusive)/Seventeenth Sunday in Ordinary Time

Proper 13 (Sunday between July 31 and August 6 inclusive)/Eighteenth Sunday in Ordinary Time

Proper 14 (Sunday between August 7 and 13 inclusive)/Nineteenth Sunday in Ordinary Time

Proper 15 (Sunday between August 14 and 20 inclusive)/ Twentieth Sunday in Ordinary Time

Proper 16 (Sunday between August 21 and 27 inclusive)/Twenty-first Sunday in Ordinary Time

Proper 17 (Sunday between August 28 and September 3 inclusive)/Twenty-second Sunday in Ordinary Time

Proper 18 (Sunday between September 4 and 10 inclusive)/Twenty-third Sunday in Ordinary Time

Proper 19 (Sunday between September 11 and 17 inclusive)/Twenty-fourth Sunday in Ordinary Time

Proper 20 (Sunday between September 18 and 24 inclusive)/Twenty-fifth Sunday in Ordinary Time

Proper 21 (Sunday between September 25 and October 1 inclusive)/Twenty-sixth Sunday in Ordinary Time

Proper 22 (Sunday between October 2 and 8 inclusive)/Twenty-seventh Sunday in Ordinary Time

Proper 23 (Sunday between October 9 and 15 inclusive)/Twenty-eighth Sunday in Ordinary Time

Proper 24 (Sunday between October 16 and 22 inclusive)/Twenty-ninth Sunday in Ordinary Time

Proper 25 (Sunday between October 23 and 29 inclusive)/Thirtieth Sunday in Ordinary Time

Proper 26 (Sunday between October 30 and November 5 inclusive)/Thirty-first Sunday in Ordinary Time

Proper 27 (Sunday between November 6 and 12 inclusive)/Thirty-second Sunday in Ordinary Time

Proper 28 (Sunday between November 13 and 19 inclusive)/Thirty-third Sunday in Ordinary Time

Proper 29 (Sunday between November 20 and 26 inclusive)/Christ the King/Last Sunday in Ordinary Time/Last Sunday after Pentecost

Explanatory Notes
for Year A, Year B, Year C
and Special Days

The explanatory notes that follow give in abbreviated form background information on the decisions to assign particular readings and psalms to the Sundays and special days in the *Common Lectionary*.

The introduction to the *Common Lectionary* provides essential information for understanding these specific explanations in light of the principles and goals of the project. For example, the "Sundays after Epiphany" should be viewed as epiphanies of Jesus, Messiah in word and deed. This period culminates on the Last Sunday after Epiphany with the proclamation of the Transfiguration gospel.

Throughout its deliberations, the CCT project committee had before it the several major three-year lectionary systems used in North America: Roman Catholic, Episcopal, Lutheran, United Methodist, Presbyterian. In many instances these different lectionary systems use the same reading, although this may sometimes vary by as little as a verse or two. When a reading for a particular day in the *Common Lectionary* is assigned to that day in all the lectionaries consulted, the explanatory note will indicate the reason for its choice as the *consensus* already existing on the reading. If the reading for a particular day in the *Common Lectionary* appears on that day in all of the lectionaries, though with slight variation in the versification, the explanatory note will indicate the reason for its choice as the *virtual consensus* already existing on the reading. An indication of *near consensus* in an explanatory note means that the reading chosen existed in the given versification in all but one of the five lectionaries on that day. When passages from denominational lectionaries seem displaced in the *Common Lectionary*, evaluators will wish to consult the Index of Scripture to see if the reading has been included on another day in this lectionary.

The explanations that follow are given by cycles of the lectionary, Year A first, followed by Year B and then Year C. This presentation will give evaluators a greater sense of the flow of the readings through a particular year of the lectionary. This should be especially helpful when the readings follow semi-continuously.

Year A

First Sunday of Advent
Isaiah 2:1-5
Psalm 122
Romans 13:11-14
Matthew 24:36-44

First reading-consensus. The psalm as a psalm of ascent celebrates Jerusalem as the focus of the Messianic fulfillment and reign of peace anticipated in the first reading. Second reading - virtual consensus. Verses 8-10 are not included since they actually relate to the earlier portion of the chapter. Third reading - consensus. Verse 36 is the proper place to begin despite the theological problem it presents.

Second Sunday of Advent
Isaiah 11:1-10
Psalm 72:1-8
Romans 15:4-13
Matthew 3:1-12

First reading-consensus. This is a messianic prophecy concerning Jesse's offspring. The royal psalm seeks God's gifts for the anointed one as a minister of justice and peace. Second reading-virtual consensus. Verses 10-13 relate the reading to the first reading and serve to emphasize hope. Third reading-consensus.

Third Sunday of Advent
Isaiah 35:1-10
Psalm 146:5-10
James 5:7-10
Matthew 11:2-11

First reading-virtual consensus. Verses 7-9 provide good Advent themes and their restoration theme stands on its own. Also, without these intervening verses the concluding verse (10) comes in too abruptly. This restoration psalm picks up the theme of deliverance in the first reading and describes it in terms of nature and human health. Second reading-consensus. Third reading-consensus.

Fourth Sunday of Advent
Isaiah 7:10-16
Psalm 24
Romans 1:1-7
Matthew 1:18-25

55

First reading-virtual consensus. Verses 10-14 provide good typology, and verses 15-16 give adequate historical context without getting into the shift to prophecy of destruction in verse 17. This first reading gives the promise of the Messiah's birth. The psalm is a psalm of praise and ascent that acknowledges God's transcendence and immanence. Second reading-consensus. Third reading-virtual consensus.

Christmas, First Proper (A,B,C)   Isaiah 9:2-7
(Christmas Eve/Day)   Psalm 96
                                            Titus 2:11-14
                                            Luke 2:1-20

First reading-consensus. The psalm proclaims the universal significance of the savior announced as the new Davidic King-Messiah in the first reading. Second reading-consensus. Verse 15 is unnecessarily negative. Third reading-consensus. Verses 15-20 round out the proclamation contained in the passage.

Christmas, Second Proper (A,B,C)   Isaiah 62:6-7, 10-12
(Additional lessons for Christmas Day)   Psalm 97
                                            Titus 3:4-7
                                            Luke 2:8-20

First reading-virtual consensus. Verses 8-9 are unnecessary. This reading is an exhortation to prepare for God's salvation. The psalm testifies to the joy and justice of that salvation. Second reading-virtual consensus. Since the third reading does not begin before verse 8, it avoids repetition of all the verses in Christmas First Proper (Luke 2:1-20).

Christmas, Third Proper (A,B,C)   Isaiah 52:7-10
(Additional lessons for Christmas Day)   Psalm 98
                                            Hebrews 1:1-12
                                            John 1:1-14

First reading-consensus. The psalm calls all to respond with music and acclamation to the good news of redemption announced in the first reading to Zion and all the nations. Second reading-virtual consensus. Verses 7-12 round out the reading and provide a clearer relationship with the gospel. The shorter version of the third reading keeps the traditional passage intact by itself. The longer version (John 1:1-18) appears on the Second Sunday after Christmas.

First Sunday After Christmas   Isaiah 63:7-9
                                         Psalm 111
                                         Hebrews 2:10-18
                                         Matthew 2:13-15, 19-23

The first reading complements the "flight to Egypt" story of the gospel. This reading recounts the saving goodness of God, even in the midst of affliction. The psalm sings of this salvation and calls all to the wisdom which begins with fearing God. The passion coloring of the Matthew narrative is alluded to in the second reading, which depicts Jesus taking on flesh in order to suffer. Third reading-near consensus. John 1:1-14 already appears on Christmas, Third Proper, and John 1:1-18 on Second Sunday after Christmas.

January 1-Holy Name of Jesus;	Numbers 6:22-27
Solemnity of Mary, Mother of God	Psalm 67
(A,B,C)	Galatians 4:4-7
	or Philippians 2:9-13
	Luke 2:15-21

January 1-When observed as New Year	Deuteronomy 8:1-10
(Eve or Day)	Psalm 117
	Revelation 21:1-6a
	Matthew 25:31-46

The readings were adopted from the Presbyterian lectionary for use on New Year's Eve or day. The psalm praises God for the love and faithfulness shown to his chosen people in the commands and promise rehearsed in the first reading.

Second Sunday After Christmas (A,B,C)	Jeremiah 31:7-14
	or Ecclesiasticus 24:1-4,
	12-16
	Psalm 147:12-20
	Ephesians 1:3-6, 15-18
	John 1:1-18

Jeremiah is the festal restoration lesson associated with Christmas. Ecclesiasticus picks up the wisdom theme of the John passage.

Epiphany (A,B,C)	Isaiah 60:1-6
	Psalm 72:1-14
	Ephesians 3:1-12
	Matthew 2:1-12

First reading-consensus. It ends appropriately at verse 6 with its mention of gold and frankincense. It speaks of light and glory in the sight of all nations. The psalm describes the response of all to a kingdom of justice and peace. Second reading-virtual consensus. It is the old Epiphany epistle, it is the most inclusive, and it requires no troublesome editing. Third reading-consensus.

Baptism of the Lord	Isaiah 42:1-9
(First Sunday after Epiphany)	Psalm 29
	Acts 10:34-43
	Matthew 3:13-17

First reading-virtual consensus. Verse 5 sets the stage for the following verses and verse 9 announces the new things which are inaugurated with Jesus' baptism. This passage is one of the "servant songs," and is prophetic of Jesus' messianic ministry. The psalm speaks of the word as the "voice" of God over the waters (of Jesus' baptism) and over the whole earth. Second reading-virtual consensus. Verses 39-43 conclude with mention of the forgiveness of sins in the name of Christ, a baptismal theme. The references to Jesus' death in these verses should not cause concern on this feast. The feast is mysteriological, not chronological. Jesus is baptized into his full ministry, which is that of the suffering servant who will give himself to death on the cross. Third reading-consensus.

Second Sunday After Epiphany
Isaiah 49:1-7
Psalm 40:1-11
1 Corinthians 1:1-9
John 1:29-34

First reading-virtual consensus. This versification keeps the "song" in its integrity, as it appears in Holy Week. In this song the Lord's servant testifies to his calling and the Lord promises vindication. The psalm is a personal song of hope and trust. Second reading-virtual consensus. Verses 4-9 give a richer context to the reading. Third reading-virtual consensus. This versification allows for the recovery of the ancient Epiphany gospel on all three years of this Sunday (A, B, C). Thus, here we have John the Baptist. Epiphany 2-B has John 1:35-42 (Peter and Andrew), Epiphany 2-C has John 2:1-11 (Cana). John 1:43-51 should normally be used in the sanctoral.

Third Sunday After Epiphany
Isaiah 9:1-4
Psalm 27:1-6
1 Corinthians 1:10-17
Matthew 4:12-23

First reading-virtual consensus. This describes the messianic appearance as light in darkness. The psalm identifies the Lord as "light" and "help." Second reading-virtual consensus. Verses 14-16 provide some of the human aspects of Paul's ministry. Third reading-consensus. Verses 18-23 are included to give the call of the disciples.

Fourth Sunday After Epiphany
Micah 6:1-8
Psalm 37:1-11
1 Corinthians 1:18-31
Matthew 5:1-12

First reading-near consensus. Micah is a more significant passage than that from Zephaniah. Micah contains the great exhortation to "do justice and to love kindness, and to walk humbly with God." The psalm counsels trust, patience, and meekness. Second reading-virtual consensus. Verses 18-25 seem to include the rich epiphany of the cross. Third reading - the second part of verse 12 maintains the sense of the passage.

Fifth Sunday After Epiphany

Isaiah 58:3-9a
Psalm 112:4-9
1 Corinthians 2:1-11
Matthew 5:13-16

First reading-near consensus. Beginning with verse 3 makes it possible to include the important context of identification with the poor as the reason for fasting. It is also the beginning of the subject-address. This passage ends with verse 9a because verse 10 is repetitive. This reading contrasts right behavior to legalism. The psalm describes righteousness in the same terms: "Light rises in the darkness..." Second reading-virtual consensus. Verses 6-11 express the epiphany of revelation. The third reading concludes at verse 16 since verses 17-20 introduce a new idea which obscures the connection with the first reading. These several verses are picked up on 6 Epiphany.

Sixth Sunday After Epiphany

Deuteronomy 30:15-20
or Ecclesiasticus 15:15-20
Psalm 119:1-8
1 Corinthians 3:1-9
Matthew 5:17-26

For the first reading, Deuteronomy was given preference in deference to the Churches which do not use the Apocrypha (Deuterocanonical Books) and because of the historical priority of Deuteronomy. This reading challenges God's people to choose between "life and good, death and evil." The psalm selection begins a lengthy song in praise of God's "righteous ordinances." Although 1 Cor. 2:6-10 (11-13) constituted a virtual consensus for the second reading, these verses have been used on the preceding Sunday. 1 Cor. 3:1-9 does not appear elsewhere in the lectionary and is appropriate as part of the semi-continuous reading on these Sundays. Third reading-consensus on Matthew 5. This is divided up over the next three Sundays in continuous fashion: 6 Epiphany 5:17-26; 7 Epiphany 5:27-37; 8 Epiphany 5:38-48.

Seventh Sunday After Epiphany

Isaiah 49:8-13
Psalm 62:5-12
1 Corinthians 3:10-11, 16-23
Matthew 5:27-37

The original passage from Leviticus for this Sunday has been moved to 8 Epiphany since the corresponding gospel (Mt. 5:38-48) now appears on 8 Epiphany. The Isaiah passage was moved here from 8 Epiphany. Verses 14-15 are not included since they do not relate well to the new gospel for this day. This passage from Isaiah is a testimony to the providential and universal care of God through the covenant. The psalm speaks of the unfailing power and love of God. Second reading-virtual consensus. Verses 10-11 were added to pick up where left off on the previous week and to give an ecclesial context to the passage. Third reading-see 6 Epiphany explanation.

Eighth Sunday After Epiphany

Leviticus 19:1-2,9-18
Psalm 119:33-40
1 Corinthians 4:1-5
Matthew 5:38-48

The First and third readings were moved here from 7 Epiphany. Verses 9-16 of the Leviticus passage give the social dimension of the message in verses 17-18. This reading expresses the command to love one's neighbor. The psalm prays for wisdom in keeping the commandments. The verses of the second reading are an adequate selection in view of the strong and lengthy first and third readings. Third reading-consensus (7 Epiphany). Matthew 6:25-33 now appears on Thanksgiving Day (Year B).

Last Sunday After Epiphany
(Transfiguration)

Exodus 24:12-18
Psalm 2:6-11
2 Peter 1:16-21
Matthew 17:1-9

The Exodus passage is good for this Sunday and fairly easy to grasp. This reading tells of Moses' forty days sojourn on Sinai where he receives the law of the Lord and where he beholds the glory of God. The messianic psalm promises "the ends of the earth" to God's son. The 2 Peter text is an obvious selection ("eye witnesses of his majesty"). Verses 20-21 give a rounded meaning to the passage. Third reading-consensus.

Ash Wednesday (A, B, C)

Joel 2:1-2, 12-17a
Psalm 51:1-12
2 Corinthians 5:20b-6:2 (3-10)
Matthew 6:1-6, 16-21

First reading-virtual consensus. Verses 1-2 provide the motif of the imminence of the Day of the Lord, which lends urgency to this particular fast. Verse 17a provides a good homiletic ending ("a byword among the nations") for beginning the Lenten observance, while avoiding the political complexity of verses 18-19. This passage from Joel is a call for fasting and repentance. The psalm is a profound plea for forgiveness and offering of supplication. Second reading-virtual consensus. The reading begins at verse 20b ("We beseech you") because it would be awkward to begin with the conjunction "So" at verse 20a. Verses 3-10 may be added to round out the point of the passage, which is the ministry of reconciliation. Third reading-virtual consensus. Verses 19-21 round out the passage by providing the fundamental rationale for this view of prayer, fasting, and almsgiving.

First Sunday of Lent   Genesis 2:4b-9, 15-17, 25-3:7
                                            Psalm 130
                                            Romans 5:12-19
                                            Matthew 4:1-11

First reading-virtual consensus. Verses 4b-7 preserve the Yahwist tradition in this passage. Verses 15-17 set the scene for the fall into sin which is to follow. Verse 25 shows the primordial innocence of the pair. The psalm is a response to this account of the creation and fall of humanity. It is a penitent plea for help based on trust in the mercy of God. Second reading - virtual consensus. The conclusion of the reading with verse 19 provides a stronger homiletic ending than would continuing to the end of the chapter. Third reading-consensus.

Second Sunday of Lent   Genesis 12:1-4a (4b-8)
                                            Psalm 33:18-22
                                            Romans 4:1-5 (6-12), 13-17
                                            John 3:1-17
                                                or Matthew 17:1-9

First reading-virtual consensus. The verses in parentheses allow a fuller depiction of Abraham's obedience, but they are not essential homiletically. The reading depicts God's call to Abraham and the promise of blessing to all the families of the earth. The psalm is a profession of God's faithfulness and our trust in his help. The verses in parenthesis in the second reading provide unnecessary rabbinical material. 2 Timothy 1:1-4 appears at Proper 22-C. The John gospel keeps intact the baptismal significance of the Johannine readings in the A Cycle of Lent. Matthew 17:1-9 is provided as an alternative for those Churches that wish to maintain the tradition of reading a transfiguration gospel on this Sunday.

Third Sunday of Lent   Exodus 17:3-7
                                            Psalm 95
                                            Romans 5:1-11
                                            John 4:5-26 (27-42)

The Exodus passage with its water theme fits well into the *Heilsgeschichte* sequence of the first readings in Lent. The psalm is a call to praise, with a warning that makes reference to Meribah, the place mentioned in the first reading. Second reading-virtual consensus. Verses 1-11 were chosen rather than selections within these verses for ease of reading. Third reading-near consensus. The emphasis of this reading shifts at verse 26 so verses 27-42 were left as part of the optional long form of the reading.

Fourth Sunday of Lent   1 Samuel 16:1-13
                                            Psalm 23
                                            Ephesians 5:8-14
                                            John 9:1-41

61

The First reading is successful as part of the Lenten Old Testament series. Hosea 5:15-6:6 appears at Proper 19-C. 2 Samuel 5:1-5 appears at Proper 29-C. The psalm reflects the theme of the selection of David in the first reading, the shepherd become king. Second reading-near consensus. Third reading-virtual consensus. Though long, the whole passage has been retained for its human and dramatic sweep.

Fifth Sunday of Lent	Ezekiel 37:1-14
	Psalm 116:1-9
	Romans 8:6-11
	John 11:(1-16) 17-45

First reading-virtual consensus. Verses 12-14 alone would not do justice to the imagery and theme of death and resurrection. Thus, though the gospel is also long, use of the whole Ezekiel pericope is indicated. This reading presents the vision of dry bones in the valley and the promise that God's people will be regathered. The psalm is an acknowledgment of God's goodness, ending with the confident confession, " I will walk before the Lord in the land of the living." Second reading-near consensus. This has been kept short because of the length of the first and third readings. Romans 8:14-17 appears at Pentecost (Year C) and Trinity (Year B). Third reading-virtual consensus. The introduction to this passage, verses 1-16, is included as an option because of the overall length of the reading. The recommended selection thus begins with Jesus' arrival, verse 17, and includes the profession of faith at the end, verse 45.

Lent 6 Palm Sunday (A,B,C.)		Isaiah 50:4-9a
		Psalm 118:19-29
		Philippians 2:5-11
	A.	Matthew 21:1-11
	B.	Mark 11:1-11
		or John 12:12-16
	C.	Luke 19:28-40

The psalm and gospels for this Sunday have been provided as an alternative to those for Lent 6 when observed as Passion Sunday. They are especially for the use of Churches which do not have the tradition of reading-and-procession on this Sunday and for use as an early "said" service in the Episcopal tradition. This first reading is the obedient response of the servant of God. The psalm includes the words of praise sung as Jesus entered Jerusalem, "Blessed is he who enters in the name of the Lord." Explanations of the first and second readings are given below.

Lent 6 Passion Sunday (A,B,C)	Isaiah 50:4-9a
	Psalm 31:9-16
	Philippians 2:5-11

A.   Matthew 26:14-27:66
     or Matthew 27:11-54
B.   Mark 14:1-15:47
     or Mark 15:1-39
C.   Luke 22:14-23:56
     or Luke 23:1-49

First reading-near consensus. Isaiah 52:13-53:12 appears on Good Friday. This reading is the obedient response of the servant of God, who is confident of the Lord's help in difficulty. The psalm is a prayer for deliverance based on trust. Second reading-consensus. Third reading-near consensus. These gospel selections all begin at the beginning of the theme of conspiracy or betrayal. The alternatives in each case provide a shorter passion text.

Monday, Tuesday, Wednesday of Holy Week (A,B,C)

Readings are the same for all three years. The three selections provided from Isaiah are the first three "Servant Songs."

Monday   Isaiah 42:1-9
                                Psalm 36:5-10
                                Hebrews 9:11-15
                                John 12:1-11

First reading-consensus. This is a servant song which describes the mission of God's servant, "a light to the nations." The psalm extols the goodness and graciousness of God, "In thy light do we see light." Second reading-near consensus. Third reading-consensus.

Tuesday   Isaiah 49:1-7
                                Psalm 71:1-12
                                1 Corinthians 1:18-31
                                John 12:20-36

First reading-virtual consensus. This second servant song is a call to hearken to God. The psalm is a plea for help from God for deliverance from the hands of the wicked. Second reading-near consensus. Third reading - this selection avoids anti-Semiticisms in verses 37 and on. John 13 is too anticipatory of the Supper.

Wednesday   Isaiah 50:4-9a
                                Psalm 70
                                Hebrews 12:1-3
                                John 12:21-30

First reading-consensus. This is the obedient response of the servant of God. The psalm is an appeal for deliverance from persecutors. The second reading is a more successful selection than Hebrews 11:36-39, which is difficult without most of the preceding verses of chapter II. The third reading constitutes a restoration of Anglican "Spy Wednesday" (Judas). Verse 30 provides a

63

dramatic ending and verses 36-38 are more appropriate as Thursday themes. Matthew 26 occurs on the previous Sunday (Passion/Palm Sunday).

Holy Thursday (A, B, C)

Churches that wish to emphasize the foot-washing tradition of this day can use the lessons for Year A every year. These lessons represent a consensus of the Churches for Maundy Thursday. The lessons for Year A, by virtue of the second and third readings, will also suffice for Churches wishing to have a Supper lesson. In Years B and C the Supper emphasis is found in the gospel lesson. The B and C readings are drawn from the several Churches whose lectionaries provide three cycles of readings for this day.

> A. Exodus 12:1-14
> Psalm 116:12-19
> 1 Corinthians 11:23-26
> John 13:1-15

> B. Exodus 24:3-8
> Psalm 116:12-19
> 1 Corinthians 10:16-17
> Mark 14:12-26

> C. Jeremiah 31:31-34
> Psalm 116:12-19
> Hebrews 10:16-25
> Luke 22:7-20

In Year A, the first reading gives the institution of the Passover meal. Psalm 89 is used at a "Chrism" service. It is a testimony to God's faithfulness in keeping his covenants, with the covenant of David as an example. In Year B, the first reading depicts Moses accepting God's covenant. The psalm (116) reflects some of the color of the Eucharist (verses 13 and 17). In Year C, the first reading is seen as the promise of the new covenant which comes in Jesus Christ through the Eucharist. The psalm (116) reflects some of the color of the Eucharist (verses 13 and 17).

Good Friday (A,B,C)

The readings are the same for all three years.

> Isaiah 52:13-53:12
> Psalm 22:1-18
> Hebrews 4:14-16; 5:7-9
> John 18:1-19:42
> or John 19:17-30

First reading-consensus. This is the fourth servant song, about the suffering servant whom God will exalt. The psalm reflects this suffering and includes Jesus' cry from the cross, "My God, my God, why hast thou forsaken me." Second reading-near consensus. Hebrews 10:1-25 appears on Advent 4 (Year

C), Proper 28 (Year B), and Holy Thursday (Year C). Third reading: John 18-near consensus; John 19 is provided in the lectionaries of two Churches, in one as the only gospel selection, in the other as an alternate gospel.

Easter Vigil (A, B,C)

Old Testament readings and Psalms (A,B,C):

Genesis 1:1-2:2
Psalm 33
Genesis 7:1-5, 11-18; 8:6-18;
9:8-13
Psalm 46
Genesis 22:1-18
Psalm 16
Exodus 14:10-15:1
Exodus 15:1-6, 11-13, 17-18
Isaiah 54:5-14
Psalm 30
Isaiah 55:1-11
Isaiah 12:2-6
Baruch 3:9-15, 32-4:4
Psalm 19
Ezekiel 36:24-28
Psalm 42
Ezekiel 37:1-14
Psalm 143
Zephaniah 3:14-20
Psalm 98

Genesis 1-virtual consensus. Genesis 7, 8, 9-Noah and the flood as a type of baptism is traditional and most appropriate at the Easter Vigil. Genesis 22-consensus. Exodus 14, 15-virtual consensus. Verses 10-14 of chapter 14 provide the essential context of the passage. Isaiah 54-near consensus. This selection is stronger than Isaiah 4:2-6. Isaiah 55-consensus. Baruch-this selection comes from the Roman lectionary. Ezekiel 36-virtual consensus. Verses 16-24 are not included because they contain references that are obscure and difficult homiletically. Ezekiel 37—the theme of dry bones given life, opening of graves, and placing the chosen in their own land are proper to Easter Vigil as a celebration of resurrection and new life. Zephaniah 3-near consensus. The passage begins with verse 14 because verse 12 as a beginning would presume material that precedes it.

Second Reading (A,B,C)   Romans 6:3-11
                                           Psalm 114

This is a consensus selection.

Gospel   A.   Matthew 28:1-10

	B.	Mark 16:1-8
	C.	Luke 24:1-12

Matthew 28-consensus, here or Easter Day. Mark 16-consensus, here or Easter Day. Luke 24-consensus, here or Easter Day. Verses 11-12 make for the most inclusive pericope.

Easter (A, B, C)

First Reading (A,B,C)		Acts 10:34-43
		Psalm 118:14-24

Alternative First Readings:	A.	Jeremiah 31:1-6
	B.	Isaiah 25:6-9
	C.	Isaiah 65:17-25

Second Reading:	A.	Colossians 3:1-4
		or Acts 10:34-43
	B.	1 Corinthians 15:1-11
		or Acts 10:34-43
	C.	1 Corinthians 15:19-26
		or Acts 10:34-43

For Churches having a tradition of an Old Testament lesson on Easter, and which would not celebrate the Vigil, an Old Testament lesson is provided from these traditions as an alternative to the Acts reading. If the Old Testament lesson is used, the Acts reading becomes the second lesson in order to initiate the sequential reading of Acts during the fifty days of Easter. Verses 34b-36 are included in the Acts reading to preserve the entirety of Peter's kerygmatic utterance. Colossians 3-consensus. The two selections from 1 Corinthians 15 are a virtual consensus.

Gospel (A, B,C)		John 20:1-18

Alternative Gospel Selections	A.	Matthew 28:1-10
	B.	Mark 16:1-8
	C.	Luke 24:1-12

John 20-virtual consensus. Verses 10-18 are used because they include Jesus' actual appearance and the Easter proclamation. The gospel alternatives are provided in the lectionaries of several Churches. Regarding the selection from Luke, the latest biblical scholarship attests to the authenticity of verses 11-12. Verse 12 is important because it includes the scene in which Peter overcomes his disbelief.

Easter Evening (A,B,C)	Acts 5:29-32
	or Daniel 12:1-3
	Psalm 150
	1 Corinthians 5:6-8
	or Acts 5:29-32
	Luke 24:13-49

As with the readings for Easter(day), an Old Testament alternative is given for the first reading. If the Old Testament selection is used, the Acts passage is used as the second reading. The Daniel reading gives the vision of the consummation of history, the general resurrection, and judgment. The psalm of praise climaxes the book of psalms and is a fitting climax for Easter day: "Let everything that breathes praise the Lord." The gospel passage is, appropriately, the Emmaus story. Its length should not be a problem at an evening service.

Second Sunday of Easter   Acts 2:14a, 22-32
                                               Psalm 16:5-11
                                               1 Peter 1:3-9
                                               John 20:19-31

The Acts passage gives the initial proclamation of the Easter kerygma and serves to maintain the sequential reading of Acts. Acts 2:42-47 now follows this initial proclamation (Easter 4-A) since it depicts the results of the Easter kerygma. The psalm contains the section referred to by Peter in the Acts selection. Second reading-consensus. Third reading-consensus.

Third Sunday of Easter   Acts 2:14a, 36-41
                                               Psalm 116:12-19
                                               1 Peter 1:17-23
                                               Luke 24:13-35

The Acts passage is kerygmatic and shows the results of the early preaching. It maintains the sequential reading of Acts. This reading gives the response of the people to Peter's Pentecost sermon. They ask: "What shall we do?" The psalm is one of thanksgiving for the goodness of the Lord. It asks: "What shall I render to the Lord for all his bounty to me?" Second reading-virtual consensus. Verse 23 provides a more powerful ending than verse 21 or verse 25, and it includes the baptismal theme of the other readings. Third reading-consensus.

Fourth Sunday of Easter   Acts 2:42-47
                                               Psalm 23
                                               1 Peter 2:19-25
                                               John 10:1-10

The Acts passage maintains the sequential reading and is more significant than the Acts 6 material. The psalm is related to the shepherd imagery in the gospel and the brotherhood of believers depicted in Acts. Second reading-virtual consensus. Verse 19 provides a better beginning than verse 20 by giving a context for the verses that follow. Also, verse 20b would be a difficult place to begin in some versions of the Bible. Third reading-consensus.

Fifth Sunday of Easter   Acts 7:55-60
                                               Psalm 31:1-8

1 Peter 2:2-10
John 14:1-14

The Acts 7 passage has been moved here from Easter 7-C out of consideration for those Churches which will have Easter 7 as Ascension and therefore will miss the reading about Stephen. The Acts 6 passage is not as significant as this one, which corresponds to the gospel at several points: I am the way, the truth, and the life; to have seen me is to have seen the Father; etc. The story of the stoning of Stephen is followed by the psalm, which prays for deliverance from personal enemies. Second reading-virtual consensus. Since the A Cycle readings are central to the mystagogy for catechumens, verses 2-3 are important as the beginning of the passage and verse 10 provides a good ending. Third reading-virtual consensus. Verses 13-14 provide a good ending, and verse 15 begins the selection for Easter 6.

Sixth Sunday of Easter

Acts 17:22-31
Psalm 66:8-20
1 Peter 3:13-22
John 14:15-21

The Acts 17 passage seemed more significant than the Acts 8 material. In it Paul preaches in Athens on Mars' Hill. The psalm of praise contains the invitation, "Come and hear, all you who fear God, and I will tell what he has done for me." Second reading-virtual consensus. Verse 13 provides a good beginning by putting the passage in the context of trial and suffering. Verses 19-22 relate the earlier material to baptism and conclude with a reference to the Ascension, which follows. Third reading-near consensus.

Ascension (A,B,C)

Acts 1:1-11
Psalm 47
Ephesians 1:15-23
Luke 24:46-53
    or Mark 16:9-16, 19-20

First reading-consensus. The possible alternative of Daniel 7:9-14 now appears on Proper 28-B. The Acts passage is the introduction to Acts and contains the account of the Ascension of the Lord. The psalm has descriptive language that applies to the Ascension and its consequences: "God has gone up with a shout"; "God reigns over the nations." Second reading-virtual consensus. It would be difficult to begin it at verse 16 or 17. Luke gospel-near consensus. Verses 44-45 are unnecessary to this passage since they are a complement to the earlier Emmaus scene. Mark gospel, beginning with verse 9, establishes the context of the resurrectional appearances. It includes verse 16 with its reference to being baptized and saved. Matthew 28:16-20 appears on Trinity Sunday (Year A).

Seventh Sunday of Easter

Acts 1:6-14
Psalm 68:1-10

1 Peter 4:12-14; 5:6-11
John 17:1-11

Those who celebrate Ascension on this Sunday will either find sufficient Ascension material in these readings or will transfer the Ascension readings to this day. First reading-virtual consensus. Verses 1-5 are unnecessary since verses 6 and 7 suitably establish the context for Ascension and Pentecost as well as the theme of the imminence of Pentecost. This reading gives the account of the Ascension plus the disciples meeting for prayer. The psalm celebrates God's triumph and expresses confidence in God to provide for his own. Second reading-virtual consensus. Beginning with verse 12 puts our sufferings in the context of Jesus' sufferings. The conclusion with 5:6-11 provides a powerful end to the Easter readings. Third reading-virtual consensus. The whole of verse 11 provides a stronger ending than half of the verse.

Pentecost (A,B,C)

First Reading	A-B-C	Acts 2:1-21
		Psalm 104:24-34
Alternative First Reading	A.	Isaiah 44:1-8
	B.	Ezekiel 37:1-14
	C.	Genesis 11:1-9
Second Reading	A.	1 Corinthians 12:3b-13
		or Acts 2:1-21
	B.	Romans 8:22-27
		or Acts 2:1-21
	C.	Romans 8:14-17
		or Acts 2:1-21
Gospel	A.	John 20:19-23
		or John 7:37-39
	B.	John 15:26-27; 16:4b-15
	C.	John 14:8-17, 25-27

The Old Testament alternatives for the first reading are drawn from the Pentecost vigil to allow Churches that do not observe the vigil to use these readings. In this case the Acts passage, because of its privileged place on Pentecost, is used as the second reading. This expanded form of the Acts reading takes in the Joel citation. Joel 2:23-30 now appears at Proper 21 (Year C). The Isaiah 44 passage contains references to water and the Spirit, both of which come up in the John 7 reading.

The 1 Corinthians reading appears in several lectionaries. The additional half verse (verse 3b) makes the passage more inclusive and starts it with the Christological affirmation which the Spirit engenders. The new creation theme of Romans 8 is appropriate to the Acts passage as well as to Pentecost as a whole.

The John 20 passage is a near consensus. The John 15 and 16 passage is complemented by the references to the Spirit in the first two readings for Year B. The John 16 material was drawn from Trinity Sunday (Year C). These final verses to the Pentecost-B gospel round out the passage by providing the third, fourth, and fifth Paraclete sayings. The John 14 passage appears in several lectionaries on one of the three years for Pentecost. These verses provide the first and second Paraclete sayings. Although this passage is also used on Easter 6, its theological theme on that occasion is distinct from its use on Pentecost.

Trinity Sunday
Deuteronomy 4:32-40
Psalm 33:1-12
2 Corinthians 13:5-14
Matthew 28:16-20

The last verses of the Deuteronomy selection are suggestive of the great commission at the end of Matthew 28. This Old Testament reading contains a recital of God's mighty acts, to which his people are to respond. The psalm is an exhortation to praise the Lord, and it gives reasons for doing so. Second reading-virtual consensus. It contains ethical material complementary with that in Deuteronomy. Third reading-virtual consensus.

Proper 4
Genesis 12:1-9
Psalm 33:12-22
Romans 3:21-28
Matthew 7:21-29

With this first reading Year A begins its semi-continuous treatment of the Pentateuchal material, from Abraham's call to the death of Moses. For a further explanation of the semi-continuous material, see the introduction, pp. 18-25. Following upon the first reading's depiction of the call of Abraham and the covenant God made with him to make of him a great nation, the psalm begins "Blessed is the nation whose God is the Lord." Second reading-consensus. Verses 26-27 are included in order to present as a block this material by Paul. Third reading-virtual consensus. Verses 28-29 were included in order to round off the Sermon on the Mount.

Proper 5
Genesis 22:1-18
Psalm 13
Romans 4:13-18
Matthew 9:9-13

The first reading continues the story of Abraham: God's testing of him and the reiteration of the covenant. The psalm is a lament that includes a prayer for help and the assurance of deliverance. Second reading-verse 13 provides a good beginning and verse 18 a good ending to this section of Romans. Third reading-consensus.

Proper 6   Genesis 25:19-34
                                            Psalm 46
                                            Romans 5:6-11
                                            Matthew 9:35-10:8

First reading is the story of the birth of Esau and Jacob, of their rivalry and the selling of the birthright to Jacob. The psalm expresses faith that God will keep his people, even in difficulties. Its usual refrain is "The God of Jacob is our refuge." Second reading-consensus. Third reading-virtual consensus. Verse 8 is an appropriate ending, with Jesus telling his disciples to do as he has done.

Proper 7   Genesis 28:10-17
                                            Psalm 91:1-10
                                            Romans 5:12-19
                                            Matthew 10:24-33

The first reading is the story of Jacob's dream at Bethel in which the Lord is revealed as the God of Abraham and Isaac, and becomes Jacob's God. The psalm expresses the conviction that those who trust in the Lord need fear no peril. Second reading-virtual consensus. The burden of the argument is contained in these verses and summed up in verses 18-19. Third reading-virtual consensus. Verse 24 is necessary since it presents the premise for the conclusion contained in verse 26.

Proper 8   Genesis 32:22-32
                                            Psalm 17:1-7, 15
                                            Romans 6:3-11
                                            Matthew 10:34-42

The first reading is the account of Jacob wrestling with the angel and being renamed Israel. The psalm is a prayer for deliverance which ends with an expression of confidence in the Lord: "As for me, I shall behold thy face in righteousness." Second reading-virtual consensus. Verses 1 and 2 are not a necessary part of this witness of Paul on baptism. Third reading-virtual consensus. Verse 34 is an appropriate beginning since this is where the thought begins.

Proper 9   Exodus 1:6-14, 22—2:10
                                            Psalm 124
                                            Romans 7:14-25a
                                            Matthew 11:25-30

The first reading is about Joseph's death, the beginning of the bondage in Egypt, and the birth of Moses and provision for his safety and care. The psalm is a thanksgiving for deliverance. The second reading deals theologically with the "fall" and is used here because it does not appear elsewhere in the lectionary and fits into the semi-continuous reading of Romans. Third reading—consensus.

Proper 10
                                           Exodus 2:11-22
Psalm 69:6-15
Romans 8:9-17
Matthew 13:1-9, 18-23

The first reading depicts Moses' identification with his people and his subsequent flight to Midian after killing the Egyptian. The psalm describes a problem similar to that of Moses: "I have become a stranger to my brethren. Zeal for thy house has consumed me," and "With thy faithful help rescue me." Second reading—this passage follows easily and well after the selection on the previous Sunday. Verses 6-11 now appear at Lent 5-A. Third reading—virtual consensus.

Proper 11
                                           Exodus 3:1-12
Psalm 103:1-13
Romans 8:18-25
Matthew 13:24-30, 36-43

The first reading depicts the call of Moses to return to Egypt and lead his people. The psalm is an exhortation to bless the Lord because of his mercy as seen in the fact that "The Lord works vindication and justice for all who are oppressed. He made known his ways to Moses, his acts to the people of Israel." Second reading—this and the selections from Romans on the following two Sundays provide major blocks of material from Romans 8. Verses 26-30 now appear on the next Sunday, Proper 12. Third reading—near consensus.

Proper 12
                                           Exodus 3:13-20
Psalm 105:1-11
Romans 8:26-30
Matthew 13:44-52

The first reading shows God commissioning Moses to return to Egypt to lead his people to the promised land. The psalm is a call to give thanks to God for all he has done. It climaxes with the promise "To you I will give the land of Canaan, as your portion for an inheritance." Second reading-virtual consensus. Third reading-virtual consensus.

Proper 13
                                           Exodus 12:1-14
Psalm 143:1-10
Romans 8:31-39
Matthew 14:13-21

The first reading gives the institution of the Passover. The psalm describes a celebration such as the Passover: "I remember the days of old, I meditate on all that thou hast done, I muse on what thy hands have wrought." Second reading—near consensus. Third reading— consensus.

Proper 14

Exodus 14:19-31
Psalm 106:4-12
Romans 9:1-5
Matthew 14:22-33

The first reading depicts the crossing of the sea by God's people. The psalm is a recital of God's faithfulness despite the unfaithfulness of the people, with particular reference made to the crossing of the sea. Second reading—consensus. Third reading—consensus.

Proper 15

Exodus 16:2-15
Psalm 78:1-3, 10-20
Romans 11:13-16, 29-32
Matthew 15:21-28

The first reading contains the complaint of the people in the desert, their longing to return to Egypt, and God's provision of food for them. The psalm is a call to hear what God says and a recital of what God has done. One of these was the provision of food and water in the desert. Second reading—virtual consensus. Third reading—consensus.

Proper 16

Exodus 17:1-7
Psalm 95
Romans 11:33-36
Matthew 16:13-20

The first reading shows again the people complaining and asking for water, which the Lord then provides from the rock at Massah and Meribah. The psalm is a call to worship God as "The rock of our salvation," with a warning not to harden hearts as at Meribah and Massah. Second reading—consensus. Third reading—consensus.

Proper 17

Exodus 19:1-9
Psalm 114
Romans 12:1-13
Matthew 16:21-28

The first reading shows God appearing to Moses, telling him to remind the people of what God has done and of the covenant. The psalm is a hymn of praise to God for creating his people. Second reading—near consensus on verses 1-8. Verses 9-13 are important and do not appear elsewhere in the lectionary. Third reading—virtual consensus. Verse 28 makes it possible to read through the canonical pericope.

Proper 18

Exodus 19:16-24
Psalm 115:1-11
Romans 13:1-10
Matthew 18:15-20

The first reading shows Moses meeting God on Mount Sinai, where he is instructed to bring Aaron with him. The psalm contrasts the Lord's power and the powerlessness of pagan idols. In verse 10 the people are addressed as "the house of Aaron." Second reading—this whole passage is a classic in Christian history. Verses 1-7 require proper interpretation. Third reading—consensus.

Proper 19   Exodus 20:1-20
                                                 Psalm 19:7-14
                                                 Romans 14:5-12
                                                 Matthew 18:21-35

The first reading presents the decalogue. The psalm expresses praise for the revelation of God's will and ends with a prayer for preservation from evil. Second reading—near consensus on beginning with verse 5. Verse 12 provides an appropriate conclusion. Third reading—consensus

Proper 20   Exodus 32:1-14
                                                 Psalm 106:7-8, 19-23
                                                 Philippians 1:21-27
                                                 Matthew 20:1-16

The first reading depicts the making of the golden calf, God's angry reaction, and Moses' intercession for the people. The psalm gives a recital of God's deeds and refers specifically to the incident of the golden calf. Second reading—near consensus. Verses 3-11 now appear at Advent 2-C. Third reading—virtual consensus.

Proper 21   Exodus 33:12-23
                                                 Psalm 99
                                                 Philippians 2:1-13
                                                 Matthew 21:28-32

The first reading is a prayer of Moses for himself and for the people. The psalm praises God as the ruler of the earth, concerned for justice and faithful to his people. Second reading—virtual consensus. Third reading—consensus.

Proper 22   Numbers 27:12-23
                                                 Psalm 81:1-10
                                                 Philippians 3:12-21
                                                 Matthew 21:33-43

The first reading contains the call and commissioning of Joshua as Moses' successor. The psalm is a summons to worship God for delivering the people from Egypt, and it includes a reference to Meribah, which also comes up in the first reading. Second reading—this is important Pauline material (Philippians 4:1-9 now appears on the next Sunday, Proper 23-A). Third reading-consensus.

Proper 23   Deuteronomy 34:1-12
                                             Psalm 135:1-14
                                             Philippians 4:1-9
                                             Matthew 22:1-14

The first reading contains the death of Moses. The psalm gives praise for God's mighty deeds, particularly the deliverance from Egypt at the time of Moses. Second reading—this maintains the sequential reading of Philippians. Verses 4-9 appear at Advent 3-C. Third reading—consensus.

Proper 24   Ruth 1:1-19a
                                             Psalm 146
                                             1 Thessalonians 1:1-10
                                             Matthew 22:15-22

The first reading begins three successive Sundays of Ruth. This gives the story of Naomi's troubles, her decision to return to her homeland, and Ruth's decision to accompany her. The psalm praises the Lord for his help, citing the fact that he "watches over the sojourners, he upholds the widow and fatherless." Second reading—virtual consensus. Verses 6-10 were included as helpful to the passage. Third reading—consensus. Verse 22 is included as the end of the pericope.

Proper 25   Ruth 2:1-13
                                             Psalm 128
                                             1 Thessalonians 2:1-8
                                             Matthew 22:34-46

The first reading depicts Ruth gathering grain in the fields of Boaz and their meeting. The psalm is an acknowledgment of the blessing of God that comes to an individual, a family, and a nation. Second reading—this continues the sequential reading (1 Thess. 1:110 appeared on the previous Sunday). Third reading—virtual consensus. Verses 41-46 serve to complete the chapter.

Proper 26   Ruth 4:7-17
                                             Psalm 127
                                             1 Thessalonians 2:9-13, 17-20
                                             Matthew 23:1-12

The first reading has the marriage of Ruth and Boaz and the birth of their child. The psalm is one of praise for the home and family as gifts of God. Second reading—verses 9-13 are a consensus selection and verses 17-20 are an important part of the passage. Third reading—virtual consensus.

Proper 27   Amos 5:18-24
                                             Psalm 50:7-15
                                             1 Thessalonians 4:13-18
                                             Matthew 25:1-13

With this Sunday the eschatological emphasis of the last several weeks of the liturgical year is brought out. First reading—the prophet warns about the meaning of the day of the Lord and pronounces judgment on shallow worship. The psalm indicates that God judges the intent of worship, not its outward form. Second reading—near consensus. This is a strong and clearly identifiable pericope that contains a good eschatological thrust for the end of the liturgical year. Third reading—near consensus. (Matthew 25:14-30 appears at Proper 28-A).

Proper 28   Zephaniah 1:7, 12-18
                                                  Psalm 76
                                                  1 Thessalonians 5:1-11
                                                  Matthew 25:14-30

The first reading warns that the day of the Lord is at hand, and that it is a day of judgment. The psalm celebrates God's ultimate victory over those who oppose him. Second reading—near consensus. Third reading—near consensus (Matthew 25:31-46 appears on the next Sunday, Proper 29-A).

Proper 29   Ezekiel 34:11-16, 20-24
(Christ the King)   Psalm 23
                                                  1 Corinthians 15:20-28
                                                  Matthew 25:31-46

The first reading-near consensus. Verses 17-19 are distracting and unnecessary. This reading pictures the Lord as the shepherd of his sheep, to whom his protection is promised. The psalm acknowledges the Lord as shepherd. Second reading-consensus (there seems no reason to delete verse 27). Third reading-consensus.

Year B

First Sunday of Advent   Isaiah 63:16—64:8
                                              Psalm 80:1-7
                                              1 Corinthians 1:3-9
                                              Mark 13:32-37

First reading—virtual consensus. The verses from chapter 63 provide play on "name" as well as the exilic history (verses 18-19). Ending at verse 8 serves to emphasize the "name" theme rather than the penitential note in verse 9. This reading contains a plea for the coming of God the Redeemer. The psalm calls to God as shepherd and asks for restoration and life. Second reading—virtual consensus. Since this is not a continuous reading of the epistle, the historical introduction (verses 1-2) is not necessary. Third reading—virtual consensus. The context is the whole eschatological discourse. In view of length of preceding readings, verse 32 seems good place to begin.

Second Sunday of Advent   Isaiah 40:1-11
                                              Psalm 85:8-13
                                              2 Peter 3:8-15a
                                              Mark 1:1-8

First reading—virtual consensus. Verses 6-8 are important parts of this passage. In this reading the prophet comforts Jerusalem with the promise of the coming of God. The psalm celebrates the fruits of God's providence in the fertility of nature. Second reading-virtual consensus. Verse 15a provides good conclusion and avoids editing problem of verse 18, which begins with "But." Third reading—consensus.

Third Sunday of Advent   Isaiah 61:1-4, 8-11
                                              Luke 1:46b-55
                                              1 Thessalonians 5:16-24
                                              John 1:6-8, 19-28

First reading—near consensus. Isaiah 65:17-25 appears as an alternative on Easter C. Verses 4 and 8 of chapter 61 introduce restoration themes that harmonize well with John the Baptist and that provide good Advent material. Isaiah's song of the anointed one is echoed in Mary's hymn of praise after the annunciation (this day's psalm). Second reading—virtual consensus. Verses 25-28 unnecessary since this is not a continuous reading. Third reading—consensus.

Fourth Sunday of Advent   2 Samuel 7:8-16
                                               Psalm 89:1-4, 19-24
                                               Romans 16:25-27
                                               Luke 1:26-38

First reading—virtual consensus. Verses 8-16 provide essential themes without difficul ties of a greatly edited and longer passage. In this passage, the Lord promises favor to the Davidic line. The psalm responds with song and praise. Second reading—consensus. Third reading—consensus.

Christmas, First Proper (A, B, C)
(Christmas Eve/Day)

See explanatory notes under Year A.

Christmas, Second Proper (A,B,C)
(Additional lessons for Christmas Day)

See explanatory notes under Year A.

Christmas, Third Proper (A,B,C)
(Additional lessons for Christmas Day)

See explanatory notes under Year A.

First Sunday After Christmas   Isaiah 61:10—62:3
                                               Psalm 111
                                               Galatians 4:4-7
                                               Luke 2:22-40

First reading—this speaks of the restoration and of the new name, both of which fit well with the gospel passage about the presentation of Jesus. The Isaiah passage tells of God's salvation as beginning with Zion but as intended for all nations. The psalm sings of this salvation and calls all to wisdom, which begins with fearing God. The Galatians reference to Jesus' birth under the Law complements the presentation theme of the gospel. Third reading—virtual consensus.

January 1—Holy Names of Jesus;
Solemnity of Mary, Mother of God (A,B,C)

See explanatory notes under Year A.

January 1—When observed as New Year   Ecclesiastes 3:1-13
 (Eve or Day)   Psalm 8
                                               Colossians 2:1-7
                                               Matthew 9:14-17

The readings were adopted from the Presbyterian lectionary for use on New

Year's Eve or day. The first reading tells of the universality of God's providence. The psalm sings of creation's beauty and humanity's place in creation.

Second Sunday after Christmas (A,B,C)

See explanatory notes under Year A.

Epiphany (A,B,C)

See explanatory notes under Year A.

Baptism of the Lord
(First Sunday after Epiphany)

Genesis 1:1-5
Psalm 29
Acts 19:1-7
Mark 1:4-11

Although the Genesis passage occurs at the Easter vigil, this gives it prominence on Sunday and helps to link creation and redemption. The passage depicts God's creative Word being spoken in darkness over the deep waters. The psalm tells of the power of the voice of God over the waters (of Jesus' baptism) and over the whole earth. The gospel reading says that Jesus will baptize with the Spirit. This baptism is depicted vividly in the Acts passage. The addition of verses 4-6 to the gospel makes even clearer the contrast between John and Jesus and serves to distinguish John's messianic preaching from the general tenor of his preaching.

Second Sunday after Epiphany

1 Samuel 3:1-10 (11-20)
Psalm 63:1-8
1 Corinthians 6:12-20
John 1:35-42

First reading—virtual consensus. Verse 1 provides the best beginning to the passage and verses 11-20 are included as an option when the purpose of Samuel's call is considered important to the reading. This call takes place in the temple. The psalm recalls the glory of God's sanctuary in the midst of the wilderness. Second reading—virtual consensus. Verse 12 provides a good beginning and a strong one. The gospel is well suited to the CCT approach to the Sundays after Epiphany, which are to be epiphanies of Jesus as the Messiah culminating in the Transfiguration on Last Sunday after Epiphany.

Third Sunday after Epiphany

Jonah 3:1-5, 10
Psalm 62:5-12
1 Corinthians 7:29-31 (32-35)
Mark 1:14-20

First reading—near consensus. This passage is important since it is the only Jonah pericope in the Sunday lectionary. This reading depicts Jonah's call to repentance and Nineveh's response. The psalm speaks of waiting for and trusting in the forgiving love of God. Second reading—near consensus. This is good epiphanic material. The use of verses 32-35 here avoids difficulty of their possible use on Epiphany 4-B and frees that Sunday for the use of 1 Corinthians 8:1-13. Third reading—virtual consensus. Verses 21-22 are unnecessary.

Fourth Sunday after Epiphany   Deuteronomy 18:15-20
                                            Psalm 111
                                            1 Corinthians 8:1-13
                                            Mark 1:21-28

First reading—virtual consensus. In this reading God promises prophets for the people. In the psalm the holy people are given assurance of the providence and care of God. Second reading—near consensus. 1 Corinthians 7:32-35 appears as option on previous Sunday. Third reading—consensus.

Fifth Sunday after Epiphany   Job 7:1-7
                                           Psalm 147:1-11
                                           1 Corinthians 9:16-23
                                           Mark 1:29-39

First reading—near consensus. 2 Kings 4:8-17 now appears at Proper 11-C. The Job passage laments the inevitability of human suffering. The psalm recalls God's care for the "broken-hearted" and "downtrodden." Second reading—virtual consensus. Verses 20-21 are essential to the passage. Third reading—consensus.

Sixth Sunday after Epiphany   2 Kings 5:1-14
                                           Psalm 32
                                           1 Corinthians 9:24-27
                                           Mark 1:40-45

The prophetic quality of the 2 Kings passage seems preferable in this instance to the legal concerns of Leviticus 13. This 2 Kings passage recounts the healing and cleansing of Naaman the Syrian. The psalm thanks God for forgiveness. The second reading has good content and unity and was preferred to 1 Corinthians 10:31—11:1. Third reading— consensus.

Seventh Sunday after Epiphany   Isaiah 43:18-25
                                             Psalm 41
                                             2 Corinthians 1:18-22
                                             Mark 2:1-12

First reading—virtual consensus. Verse 18 begins the Oracle; verse 20 provides important pictorial imagery; and verse 25 is important in relation to the gospel. This reading from Isaiah identifies the "new thing" that God is doing as forgiveness. The psalm is a personal plea for restitution and help in trouble and rejection. Second reading—consensus. Third reading—consensus.

Eighth Sunday after Epiphany

Hosea 2:14-20
Psalm 103:1-13
2 Corinthians 3:1-6
Mark 2:18-22

First reading—virtual consensus. 2 Corinthians 3:17-4:2 now appears at Last Epiphany-C. Third reading—consensus.

Last Sunday after Epiphany
(The Transfiguration)

2 Kings 2:1-12a
Psalm 50:1-6
2 Corinthians 4:3-6
Mark 9:2-9

The 2 Kings passage relates well to the gospel. This is the story of Elijah's assumption into heaven in a chariot of fire. The psalm likens God to "a devouring fire." The 2 Corinthians passage was transferred here from Year C (Last Epiphany) to open up that day for 2 Corinthians 3:12—4:2, which is a midrash on Exodus 34 assigned to Year C. Third reading—near consensus. Verse 9 makes an appropriate ending as a pre-Easter climax.

Ash Wednesday (A,B,C)

See explanatory notes under Year A.

First Sunday of Lent

Genesis 9:8-17
Psalm 25:1-10
1 Peter 3:18-22
Mark 1:9-15

First reading—near consensus. Genesis 22:1-18 now appears at Proper 5-A. The Genesis 9 passage depicts the covenant with Noah in which God promised never again to destroy the earth. In the psalm we pray on the basis of God's promise that we may be shown his ways and walk in them. Second reading—near consensus. Romans 8:31-39 appears at Proper 13-A. Third reading—virtual consensus. Verses 9-11 serve to put the passage into the context of Jesus' baptism. Verses 14-15 round out Mark's introduction and present a stirring call to repentance.

Second Sunday of Lent

Genesis 17:1-10, 15-19
Psalm 105:1-11
Romans 4:16-25
Mark 8:31-38
  or Mark 9:1-9

The passage from Genesis 17 maintains the central covenant figures of Abraham and Sarah and, therefore, the baptismal reference, without the confusion caused by the depiction of God asking Abraham for human sacrifice. Verses 15-18 help to refocus the emphasis of the passage on covenant. Genesis 22:1-18 appears at the Easter Vigil and Genesis 28:10-17 appears at Proper 7-A. The psalm is an expression of thanks to God and encouragement to call on him, to remember "the covenant he made with Abraham." The Romans passage makes direct reference to Abraham and his faith in the promise of God. Romans 8:31-39 appears at Proper 13-A. In the third reading, the reference to the cross is baptismal since the elect are signed on the forehead with the cross at baptism. Mark 9:1-9 is provided as an alternative for those Churches that wish to maintain the tradition of reading a transfiguration gospel on this Sunday.

Third Sunday of Lent

Exodus 20:1-17
Psalm 19:7-14
1 Corinthians 1:22-25
John 2:13-22

First reading—consensus. This contains the Decalogue. The psalm gives praise for the revelation of God's will and ends with a prayer for preservation from evil. Second reading—near consensus. Romans 7:13-25 appears at Proper 9-A. Third reading—virtual consensus. Verses 23-25 are editorial and extraneous to the passage.

Fourth Sunday of Lent

2 Chronicles 36:14-23
Psalm 137:1-6
Ephesians 2:4-10
John 3:14-21

First reading—near consensus. Numbers 21:4-9 appears on Holy Cross (September 14). The 2 Chronicles passage summarizes what led to the exile to Babylon. The psalm is a part of a hymn that the exiles sang in Babylon urging the remembrance of Jerusalem. Second reading—virtual consensus. Verses 1-3 are unnecessary since duplicated in verse 4-10. Third reading—near consensus. John 6:14-15 appears at Proper 12-B.

Fifth Sunday of Lent

Jeremiah 31:31-34
Psalm 51:10-17
Hebrews 5:7-10
John 12:20-33

First reading—consensus. This gives the promise of the new covenant written on the heart. The psalm prays "Create in me a clean heart. . . ." Second reading—virtual consensus. Verses 1-6 appear at Proper 25-B. Third reading—consensus.

Lent 6 (when observed as Palm Sunday) (A,B,C)

See explanatory notes under Year A.

Lent 6 (when observed as Passion Sunday) (A,B,C)

See explanatory notes under Year A.

Monday, Tuesday, Wednesday of Holy Week (A,B,C)

See explanatory notes under Year A.

Holy Thursday (A,B,C)

See explanatory notes under Year A.

Good Friday (A,B,C)

See explanatory notes under Year A.

Easter Vigil (A,B,C)

See explanatory notes under Year A.

Easter (A,B,C)

See explanatory notes under Year A.

Easter Evening (A,B,C)

See explanatory notes under Year A.

Second Sunday of Easter　　　　　　　　Acts 4:32-35
　　　　　　　　　　　　　　　　　　　　Psalm 133
　　　　　　　　　　　　　　　　　　　　1 John 1:1—2:2
　　　　　　　　　　　　　　　　　　　　John 20:19-31

The community emphasis of the Acts passage is complemented by the gospel. Acts 3:12-19 appears on next Sunday (Easter 3-B). The Acts 4 passage describes the unity of the first church. The psalm exclaims over the joys of harmony, "Behold, how good and pleasant it is when brothers dwell together in unity." The 1 John reading was moved from Easter 3-B, where it was too long to be read with the long gospel selection. This makes it possible to read 1 John in sequence. To achieve this, 1 John 5:1-6 now appears at Easter 6-B. There is a complementary relationship between the Thomas story of the gospel and the concrete sense references of the opening of 1 John. The community emphasis of the Acts passage is also complemented by the gospel. Third reading—near consensus. Matthew 28:16-20 appears at Trinity, Year A.

Third Sunday of Easter

Acts 3:12-19
Psalm 4
1 John 3:1-7
Luke 24:35-48

In the first reading it was felt that in the context of the whole passage verses 12-13 would not be understood as anti-Semitic. Acts 4:8-12 follows on the next Sunday (Easter 4-B). With the displacement of 1 John 5:1-6 from Easter 2-B to Easter 6-B (in order to preserve the sequence of readings), all selections from 1 John move forward one Sunday. Thus 1 John 3:1-7 was transferred from Easter 4-B. Clear development of thought takes place in verses 1-7, and verse 7 provides a stronger ending than verse 3. Third reading— virtual consensus. Verse 48 provides a good homiletic ending.

Fourth Sunday of Easter

Acts 4:8-12
Psalm 23
1 John 3:18-24
John 10:11-18

This selection from Acts maintains the complementary relationship between the rejection of the cornerstone and the good shepherd of the gospel passage. Verses 32-35 now appear at Easter 2-B. The psalm picks up on the shepherd theme of the gospel. As noted previously, the selections from 1 John for these Sundays have been moved forward. Thus this passage was moved here from Easter 5-B. It picks up on the "name" mentioned in Peter's preaching in Acts. Third reading—virtual consensus. Verses 17-18 serve to round out the reading with a resurrection note and complement the commandments mentioned in the second reading.

Fifth Sunday of Easter

Acts 8:26-40
Psalm 22:25-31
1 John 4:7-12
John 15:1-8

The Acts passage is missionary and deals with baptism, both of which are appropriate to the season. It depicts the conversion of the Ethiopian eunuch. The psalm says, "All the ends of the earth shall remember and turn to the Lord." The second reading was moved here from Easter 6-B. Its verses contain a composite picture of God's love for us which results in our love for one another. The mutual indwelling of verse 12 rounds out the passage in relation to the gospel (vine and branches). Third reading—near consensus. John 14:15-21 now appears at Easter 6-A.

Sixth Sunday of Easter

Acts 10:44-48
Psalm 98
1 John 5:1-6
John 15:9-17

This selection from Acts 10 maintains the sequential reading of Acts and brings out again the theme of baptism contained in the Acts passage on Easter 5-B. It begins after verses 34-43, which appear on Easter. Verses 44-48 depict the baptism of Cornelius and the other gentiles with him. The psalm contains the promise that "All the ends of the earth have seen the victory of our God." The second reading is taken from Easter 2-B. It continues the sequential reading of 1 John and complements the gospel reading. Third reading—consensus. The commission to bear fruit in this gospel passage results in the baptizing portrayed in Acts.

Ascension (A,B,C)

See explanatory notes under Year A.

Seventh Sunday of Easter	Acts 1:15-17, 21-26
	Psalm 1
	1 John 5:9-13
	John 17:11b-19

First reading—virtual consensus. Mention of Judas' bowels is left out because unnecessary. This reading depicts the replacement of Judas Iscariot with Matthias. The psalm contrasts the godly with the ungodly. The second reading provides a strong Easter ending on eternal life. The passage concludes at a proper point while maintaining the sequential reading of 1 John. Third reading—consensus.

Pentecost (A,B,C)

See explanatory notes under Year A.

Trinity Sunday	Isaiah 6:1-8
	Psalm 29
	Romans 8:12-17
	John 3:1-17

Although the Isaiah passage appears also at 5 Epiphany (C), it is well suited to Trinity Sunday. It depicts the call of Isaiah and his response, "Here am I, send me." The psalm is a summons to give glory to God that ends with a prayer for strength and peace. Second reading—virtual consensus. This passage provides an evangelical contrast (i.e., "Abba") to the first reading. Verses 12-13 help to sustain the ethical note of the passage. Third reading—near consensus. Verses 9-17 give the Nicodemus context, which is important for the background and relationship to the Old Testament. Matthew 28:16-20 appears now at Trinity-A.

Proper 4	1 Samuel 16:1-13
	Psalm 20
	2 Corinthians 4:5-12
	Mark 2:23—3:6

With this first reading Year B begins its semi-continuous treatment of the narrative of David, from his anointing to his death. For a further explanation of the semi-continuous material, see the introduction, pp. 18-25. This passage depicts David's anointing by Samuel, which was an indication that David did not rise from the ranks but was chosen by God. The psalm is a liturgy for the king. It prays for his welfare and expresses confidence in God's help. Second reading—virtual consensus. Verse 5 with its immediate mention of Christ picks up the link between David in the first reading and Christ in the third. Third reading—virtual consensus. This long form of the gospel includes a reference to and picks up the death/life note in the second reading in terms of Jesus' healing.

Proper 5
1 Samuel 16:14-23
Psalm 57
2 Corinthians 4:13—5:1
Mark 3:20-35

In the first reading David respects God's choice of Saul and cheers Saul when depressed. The psalm is a lament, a prayer for deliverance from enemies, and it expresses confidence that this deliverance will come to pass. Second reading—virtual consensus. This selection is the most inclusive of the variants. Third reading—consensus.

Proper 6
2 Samuel 1:1,17-27
Psalm 46
2 Corinthians 5:6-10, 14-17
Mark 4:26-34

The first reading depicts David's devotion to his king and to his friend. It contains David's lament over the deaths of Saul and Jonathan. The psalm is an expression of confidence in God's continuing presence and help. The second reading is a conflation of the two passages from 2 Corinthians used on Propers 6 and 7. Verses 16 and 17 serve to parallel the passage with the gospel. These verses speak of Christ's death and the gospel speaks of the mustard seed, as a symbol of Christ's death, which must fall to the ground to come to new life. Third reading—consensus.

Proper 7
2 Samuel 5:1-12
Psalm 48
2 Corinthians 5:18—6:2
Mark 4:35-41

In the first reading David becomes king of Judah and king of Israel and establishes Jerusalem as the capital city. The psalm celebrates the beauty and security of Zion, with Jerusalem built on one of its hills. Although the latter verses of the 2 Corinthians passage appear on Ash Wednesday, they merit reading more than once in the year. They are used in a different context here and serve to highlight the "favorable time" signified by Christ's stilling of the waves in the gospel. Third reading—virtual consensus.

Proper 8   2 Samuel 6:1-15
                                                 Psalm 24
                                                 2 Corinthians 8:7-15
                                                 Mark 5:21-43

In the first reading David brings the ark of the covenant to Jerusalem, thereby linking the religious symbol of the tribal federation with his monarchy. The psalm is a liturgy which was used on entering the sanctuary. It praises the Lord as creator and sings of the entry of the king of glory. Second reading—virtual consensus. In view of length of other readings, verses 1-6 would make this passage too long. Third reading—virtual consensus. This is the most comprehensive selection of those used in the various lectionaries.

Proper 9   2 Samuel 7:1-17
                                                 Psalm 89:20-37
                                                 2 Corinthians 12:1-10
                                                 Mark 6:1-6

In the first reading David plans to build a house for God. Through the oracle of Nathan God promises instead to make a house for David, thereby indicating the divine origin of the Davidic dynasty. The psalm is a recital of God's promises to David and his seed. Second reading—virtual consensus. It begins with verse 1 in order to pick up on the revelations mentioned in verse 7. Third reading—consensus.

Proper 10   2 Samuel 7:18-29
                                                 Psalm 132:11-18
                                                 Ephesians 1:1-10
                                                 Mark 6:7-13

The first reading is David's prayer in response to God's promise to build him a house. The psalm is a recital of the Lord's promise to David. Second reading—virtual consensus. This shorter selection is sufficient and compensates for the lengthened first reading. Verses 1 and 2 are necessary in order to give the context of the passage. Third reading—consensus.

Proper 11   2 Samuel 11:1-15
                                                 Psalm 53
                                                 Ephesians 2:11-22
                                                 Mark 6:30-34

The first reading is the story of David's sin with Bathsheba and against Uriah. The psalm describes human wickedness, God's punishment, and ends with a prayer for deliverance. Second reading—virtual consensus. This longer version of the Ephesians passage preserves the contrast of the pre-covenant situation with the reality for believing Gentiles after Christ. Third reading—consensus. Because of the long preceding readings, this short gospel is effective. The reference in verse 34 to the shepherd is important, especially in light of the miracle of the feeding picked up in the John 6 gospel on the next Sunday.

Proper 12   2 Samuel 12:1-14
                                                 Psalm 32
                                                 Ephesians 3:14-21
                                                 John 6:1-15

The first reading depicts the uncovering of David's sin and his repentance. The psalm is penitential. It conveys confession, forgiveness, and an exhortation to repent. The Ephesians 3 passage with its famous doxology is included here since it does not otherwise appear in the Sunday lectionary. Ephesians 4:1-6 is moved to the following Sunday, Proper 13-B. Third reading—near consensus.

Proper 13   2 Samuel 12:15b-24
                                                 Psalm 34:11-22
                                                 Ephesians 4:1-6
                                                 John 6:24-35

The first reading depicts the death of the first child of Bathsheba, David's repentance, and the birth of Solomon. The psalm is a warning against sin and an assurance of the deliverance of God. The Ephesian passage was moved here from the preceding Sunday. Ephesians 4:17-24 was dropped from the lectionary. Third reading—consensus.

Proper 14   2 Samuel 18:1, 5, 9-15
                                                 Psalm 143:1-8
                                                 Ephesians 4:25—5:2
                                                 John 6:35, 41-51

The first reading is part of the Succession Narrative, which sketches the traditions about attempts by David's sons to seize the throne. In this passage Absalom is killed despite David's orders to deal gently with him. The psalm is a prayer for deliverance from personal enemies. Second reading—virtual consensus. The earlier verses in the Ephesians passage make an interesting match with 2 Samuel "do not be angry" and "deal gently"). Third reading—virtual consensus. Verse 35 is necessary in order to provide the context for the response of those present (verse 41) to the statement of Jesus about being the "bread of life."

Proper 15   2 Samuel 18:24-33
                                                 Psalm 102:1-12

Ephesians 5:15-20
John 6:51-58

In the first reading David receives the news of Absalom's death and mourns his son. This passage presents the problem of the succession and why Solomon succeeded David. The psalm is the prayer of one who is afflicted, but who yet praises God. Second reading— consensus. Third reading—virtual consensus. The inclusion of verse 51 provides the remark of Jesus that gives rise to the dispute that follows.

Proper 16

2 Samuel 23:1-7
Psalm 67
Ephesians 5:21-33
John 6:55-69

The first reading gives the last words of David. He compares God's care for his people with the sun and the rain that make the grass grow. The psalm is one of thanksgiving for the harvest and is applicable to all of God's blessings. Second reading—virtual consensus. This is a self-contained theological piece. Third reading—virtual consensus. This passage overlaps with the previous Sunday by beginning at verse 55 in order to pick up the reason for the difficulty of the disciples.

Proper 17

1 Kings 2:1-4, 10-12
Psalm 121
Ephesians 6:10-20
Mark 7:1-8, 14-15, 21-23

The first reading gives David's charge to Solomon, the account of David's death, and Solomon's ascension to the throne of David. The psalm is a song of praise to the Lord who is the giver of help and who protects from all evil. The Ephesians material concludes on this Sunday. James 1:17-27 now appears on the following Sunday, Proper 18-B. Third reading-consensus.

Proper 18

Ecclesiasticus 5:8-15
or Proverbs 2:1-8
Psalm 119:129-136
James 1:17-27
Mark 7:31-37

The Davidic narrative concluded on the previous Sunday. Several Sundays of Wisdom literature now follow. The Isaiah 35 material appears on Advent 3-A. The Ecclesiasticus text is wisdom about life and behavior, particularly in speaking. This works well with "hearers of the Word" in the James passage that follows and with the hearing miracle in the gospel. The Proverbs reading is provided as an alternative for Churches that do not use Ecclesiasticus. The Proverbs text describes the fruits of seeking the wisdom that the Lord gives. The James reading was moved here from the preceding Sunday.

The material from James 2 now appears on the following Sunday, Proper 19-B. Third reading— consensus.

Proper 19

Proverbs 22:1-2, 8-9
Psalm 125
James 2:1-5, 8-10, 14-17
Mark 8:27-38

The first reading displaces Isaiah 50:4-9a, which appears at Lent 6 (Palm/Passion Sunday). The Proverbs passage tells of the value of a good name and the virtue of sharing with others. The psalm is an expression of confidence in God and a prayer for God's blessing. The James passage was moved here from the preceding Sunday. It concludes at verse 17 because verse 18 would be a weak ending. Third reading—virtual consensus. The longer version of the gospel was chosen because the first reading is short.

Proper 20

Job 28:20-28
Psalm 27:1-6
James 3:13-18
Mark 9:30-37

Wisdom 2 and Jeremiah 11 were displaced in favor of Job 28, which gives the central statement of Wisdom. This passage identifies wisdom as the property of God, but accessible to humanity. The psalm is a song of trust in the Lord. The James passage includes only verses from chapter 3 because chapter 4 introduces a new subject. Third reading— consensus.

Proper 21

Job 42:1-6
Psalm 27:7-14
James 4:13-17, 5:7-11
Mark 9:38-50

The first reading displaces Numbers 11. In this passage Job gives answer to the Lord after considering what the Lord has done. The psalm is a prayer spoken in time of trouble in response to the goodness of the Lord. The new pericope from James seemed preferable. Third reading—virtual consensus. The final verses include a wisdom-like proverb on salt.

Proper 22

Genesis 2:18-24
Psalm 128
Hebrews 1:1-4, 2:9-11
Mark 10:2-16

First reading—consensus. This passage depicts the creation of woman and the institution of marriage. The psalm is a recital of the blessings of the Lord, including that of the family. This Sunday begins the semi-continuous reading of Hebrews. The addition of the four initial verses to this passage provides an introduction to this semi-continuous presentation. These verses help to establish a theological continuity in the Christ who was once lower and is now exalted. The later verses seem unnecessary. Third reading—virtual consensus. This is the most comprehensive of the versions used on this Sunday.

Proper 23

Genesis 3:8-19
Psalm 90:1-12
Hebrews 4:1-3, 9-13
Mark 10:17-30

The Genesis 3 passage was removed from Proper 5-B in order to make possible the semi-continuous reading of 2 Samuel. It fits well here with the passage from Hebrews and is in sequence with the Genesis 2 reading on the previous Sunday. This reading depicts the rebellion of Adam and Eve against God. The psalm is a prayer for deliverance. It cites God's everlasting existence and our transitory nature so that we may be wise in this knowledge. The Hebrews passage avoids the elaborate midrashic discussion of psalm 95 in verses 4-8, and it provides a concrete context for statements about the Word of God. Third reading—virtual consensus. Verse 31 would add nothing to this passage.

Proper 24

Isaiah 53:7-12
Psalm 35:17-28
Hebrews 4:14-16
Mark 10:35-45

First reading—virtual consensus. This passage was considered sufficient and was kept fairly short because of the long gospel this Sunday. This is the fourth servant song: it speaks of God's judgment against sin and of God's mercy on us. The psalm is a prayer for deliverance from enemies and for vindication: "Great is the Lord, who delights in the welfare of his servant." Second reading—near consensus. It picks up where left off the previous Sunday and concludes the chapter. Third reading—consensus.

Proper 25

Jeremiah 31:7-9
Psalm 126
Hebrews 5:1-6
Mark 10:46-52

First reading—near consensus. Isaiah 59 not used because the lectionary contains more readings from Isaiah than from Jeremiah, and in this instance the Jeremiah passage serves just as well. This passage is part of the message of consolation that gives assurance of the restoration of the people. The psalm is a song of thanks for this restoration. Second reading—near consensus. This passage concludes at verse 6 because verses 7-9 already appear on Lent 5-B. Third reading—consensus.

Proper 26   Deuteronomy 6:1-9
                                                     Psalm 119:33-48
                                                     Hebrews 7:23-28
                                                     Mark 12:28-34

First reading-virtual consensus. This passage requires verse 1 for meaning
and verses 7-9 for a proper completion. It gives the purpose of the law and
enunciates the law of love of God. The psalm is a prayer to know and keep
the Lord's commandments. Second reading— consensus. Third reading—
consensus. The gospel must begin at verse 28 in order to provide the narrative context and to make sense of the scribe mentioned again in verse 34.

Proper 27   1 Kings 17:8-16
                                                     Psalm 146
                                                     Hebrews 9:24-28
                                                     Mark 12:38-44

The first reading must begin at verse 8 with the word of the Lord to Elijah.
Daniel 12:1-3 appears as the alternative first reading on Easter Evening. The
1 Kings passage shows Elijah being fed by the widow whose supplies then
never run out. The psalm tells of the wisdom of trusting God, "who gives
food to the hungry," and "upholds the widow." Second reading—near consensus. Hebrews 10:11-18 appears at Proper 28-B. Third reading—near consensus. Mark 13:24-32 appears at Proper 28-B.

Proper 28   Daniel 7:9-14
                                                     Psalm 145:8-13
                                                     Hebrews 10:11-18
                                                     Mark 13:24-32

The first reading was moved here from Proper 29-B (Christ the King). It fits
well with the selection from Hebrews. Daniel 12:1-3 appears as the alternative first reading on Easter Evening. Daniel 7 gives the vision of the kingdom
of the Son of Man. The psalm gives praise for the Lord's rule and kingdom.
The second reading picks up from previous Sunday. In the third reading,
verses 14-23 are not needed and are too connected to the historical circumstances of the writer. Verse 32 sums up what preceded.

Proper 29   Jeremiah 23:1-6
(Christ the King)   Psalm 93
                                                     Revelation 1:4b-8
                                                     John 18:33-37

The Jeremiah passage was moved from Proper 11-B in order to use the
semi-continuous Davidic material. It was already an alternative in several
lectionaries for this Sunday in Year C. It is especially appropriate to the
theme of "king" and serves to bring the Davidic strain in Year B to a conclusion. The psalm gives praise for the majesty of the Lord. Second reading—

virtual consensus. This gives the most comprehensive versification from the selections provided in the various lectionaries. Third reading—near consensus. John 1:35-42 appears on Epiphany 2-B. In John 18, verse 33 serves to provide the identity of the speaker.

Year C

First Sunday of Advent   Jeremiah 33:14-16
                                                          Psalm 25:1-10
                                                          1 Thessalonians 3:9-13
                                                          Luke 21:25-36

First reading - near consensus. This gives the promise of a "righteous branch". The psalm tells of trust in the mercy of the Lord to restore righteousness to his people. Second reading - near consensus. Verse 9 provides good beginning, and verse 13 is a strong ending. Material from chapter 4 not used since this begins a new section. 1 Thessalonians 5:1-11 now appears at Proper 28-A. Third reading - uses comprehensive versification in order to include the mention of the fig tree and the peculiarly Lucan material in verses 35-36.

Second Sunday of Advent   Baruch 5:1-9
                                                            or Malachi 3:1-4
                                                          Psalm 126
                                                          Philippians 1:3-11
                                                          Luke 3:1-6

Malachi 3 is provided as an alternative for those churches that do not use Baruch. Baruch anticipates the glory that will follow Israel's restoration. Malachi speaks of the purifying that must precede that restoration. The psalm prays for the restoration, likening it to a harvest festival. Second reading-virtual consensus. This provides the most comprehensive versification in the several lectionaries. Verse 3 is a better beginning than verse 4. Third reading-consensus.

Third Sunday of Advent   Zephaniah 3:14-20
                                                          Isaiah 12:2-6
                                                          Philippians 4:4-9
                                                          Luke 3:7-18

First reading - virtual consensus. Verses 19-20 provide a strong connection with this Sunday's gospel and contain good advent "promise" material. This passage is a Messianic acclamation. The canticle is an invitation to rejoice in the salvation of God. Second reading - virtual consensus. Verses 8-9 are good material for this passage, even though they also appear at Proper 23-A. Third reading - virtual consensus. Verse 7 picks up from the previous Sunday and serves to identify the speaker.

Fourth Sunday of Advent

Micah 5:2-5a
Psalm 80:1-7
Hebrews 10:5-10
Luke 1:39-55

First reading - consensus. This contains the promise to Bethlehem of greatness. The psalm prays for a shepherd, an anointed redeemer. Second reading - consensus. Third reading - virtual consensus. This versification includes the full canticle of Mary.

Christmas, First Proper (A, B,C)
(Christmas Eve/Day)

See explanatory notes under Year A.

Christmas, Second Proper (A,B,C)
(Additional lessons for Christmas Day)

See explanatory notes under Year A.

Christmas, Third Proper (A,B,C.)
(Additional lessons for Christmas Day)
See explanatory notes under Year A

First Sunday After Christmas

1 Samuel 2:18-20, 26
or Ecclesiasticus 3:3-7, 14-17
Psalm 111
Colossians 3:12-17
Luke 2:41-52

The 1 Samuel passage was placed here because it is the primary source for the Lucan gospel. The Ecclesiasticus reading is optional and may be used when emphasis is placed on the family. This passage speaks of familial virtues and responsibilities. The 1 Samuel reading relates such duties to the whole community of faith. The psalm is expressive of the discipline by which we respond to the faithfulness God shows to his people. The Colossians reading expounds virtues necessary to life in common. It goes well with the family elements of the gospel. Third reading - consensus.

January 1 - Holy Name of Jesus:
Solemnity of Mary, Mother of God (A, B,C)

See explanatory notes under Year A

January 1 - When observed as New Year   Isaiah 49:1-10
(Eve or Day)   Psalm 90:1-12
                                              Ephesians 3:1-10
                                              Luke 14:16-24

The readings were adopted from the Presbyterian lectionary for use on New Year's Eve or day. The first reading identifies Israel's destiny with its mission to all nations. The psalm is a confession of the eternal and unchanging care of God.

Second Sunday After Christmas (A, B,C)

See explanatory notes under Year A.

Epiphany (A, B,C)

See explanatory notes under Year A.

Baptism of the Lord
(First Sunday after Epiphany)   Isaiah 61:1-4
                                              Psalm 29
                                              Acts 8:14-17
                                              Luke 3:15-17, 21-22

The Isaiah reading goes well with the baptism of Jesus depicted in Luke 3 and it helps to prepare for the Luke 4 passage on the Third Sunday after Epiphany (C). This section of Isaiah gives a poetic description of the Messiah's ministry that Jesus assumes in his baptism and proclaims in his sermon at Nazareth. The psalm tells of the power of the voice of God over the waters (of Jesus' baptism) and over the whole earth. The Acts passage highlights the baptismal theme of Jesus' anointing with the Spirit. Third reading virtual consensus. Verse 17 emphasizes a particular aspect of Jesus' role in the eschatological fulfillment.

Second Sunday after Epiphany   Isaiah 62:1-5
                                             Psalm 36:5-10
                                             1 Corinthians 12:1-11
                                             John 2:1-11

First reading - consensus. In this reading God promises to be a husband to his people. The psalm tells of the constant love of the Lord. Second reading - virtual consensus. It begins at verse 1 in order to place the *charismata* in the context of confessing Christ, as epiphanies of the Lord. Third reading - virtual consensus. Concluding this passage at verse 11 helps to emphasize the epiphanic character of this Sunday.

Third Sunday after Epiphany   Nehemiah 8:1-4a, 5-6, 8-10
                                             Psalm 19:7-14

1 Corinthians 12:12-30
Luke 4:14-21

First reading - near consensus. Isaiah 61:1-4 appears at Baptism of the Lord (C) and at advent 3-B. The editing of the Nehemiah passage avoids the use of the difficult names it contains. This reading depicts the great day when Ezra and Nehemiah renewed respect for the law of God. The psalm gives praise for the Lord's law. Second reading - virtual consensus. This is the most comprehensive selection. It includes the body metaphor of verses 27-30. Third reading - virtual consensus. The use of chapter 1:1-4 with this selection would be confusing since the reading would then loose some of its sense.

Fourth Sunday after Epiphany
Jeremiah 1:4-10
Psalm 71:1-6
1 Corinthians 13:1-13
Luke 4:21-30

First reading - virtual consensus. With the use of verses 4-10, verses 17-19 become redundant. This passage is the account of Jeremiah's call. Jeremiah, like the psalm, confesses his dependence on God from his mother's womb. Second reading - near consensus. Chapter 12:31 would be a difficult beginning for the passage. 13:1 serves well as a beginning, emphasizing love as a gift/epiphany. Third reading - virtual consensus. Verses 31-32 are anti-climactic.

Fifth Sunday After Epiphany
Isaiah 6:1-8 (9-13)
Psalm 138
1 Corinthians 15:1-11
Luke 5:1-11

First reading - near consensus. Although Isaiah 6:1-8 also appears at Trinity Sunday (B), it was considered useful here. The prophetic message (verses 9-13) was kept as an option. These first verses of Isaiah 6 give the account of the call of Isaiah in the temple. The psalm praises God from the temple and recalls God's love for kings and for the lowly. Second reading - near consensus. Third reading - consensus.

Sixth Sunday after Epiphany
Jeremiah 17:5-10
Psalm 1
1 Corinthians 15:12-20
Luke 6:17-26

First reading - virtual consensus. Verses 9-10 complete the passage well and prepare somewhat for Lent. This passage sets out the two ways, obedience and disobedience. The first is likened, as in the psalm, to a "tree planted by water." Second reading - virtual consensus. This full form of the pericope is essential to the rather tight argument it presents. Third reading - virtual consensus. Verses 18-19 with their depiction of Jesus' healing ministry provide a good epiphamic pairing of word and deed.

Seventh Sunday after Epiphany

Genesis 45:3-11, 15
Psalm 37:1-11
1 Corinthians 15:35-38, 42-50
Luke 6:27-38

The Genesis story is better known than the other selection for this Sunday from 1 Samuel, and it needs no introduction. Verses 3-11 are sufficient with the additional essential verse 15. This is the story of the reunion of Joseph and his brothers. The psalm reflects this story in its confidence in God's providence in spite of "the wicked... wrongdoers." Second reading - virtual consensus. This versification includes the beginning of the argument with its question and the conclusion in verse 50. Third reading-consensus.

Eighth Sunday after Epiphany

Ecclesiasticus 27:4-7
or Isaiah 55:10-13
Psalm 92:1-4, 12-15
1 Corinthians 15:51-58
Luke 6:39-49

The Isaiah passage has been kept as an alternative to Ecclesiasticus for those Churches that do not use Ecclesiasticus. Jeremiah 7:1-15 did not seem to suit the gospel very well and Job 23:1-7 seemed not to apply to the gospel at all. The Ecclesiasticus passage cautions as to the test of wisdom, which the psalm expresses in praise. The reading from Isaiah speaks of the power of God's word to create the response for which it was sent forth. This response is expressed in the praise of the psalm. Second reading - virtual consensus. This passage picks up where the reading on the previous Sunday left off. Third reading - virtual consensus. Verses 46-49 serve to provide the complete sermon.

Last Sunday after Epiphany
(Transfiguration)

Exodus 34:29-35
Psalm 99
2 Corinthians 3:12-4:2
Luke 9:28-36

The passage from Exodus links nicely with the gospel's reference to Christ's "passing" (Luke 9:31). This reading narrates the appearance of Moses, with shining face, after witnessing the glory of God. The psalm's response is one of praise of God's name. The second reading was adapted from the Episcopal lectionary for Epiphany 8-B. Third reading - near consensus. Luke 23:35-43 is included in the alternative gospel for Lent 6-C (when observed as Passion Sunday)

Ash Wednesday (A, B,C)

See explanatory notes under Year A

First Sunday of Lent

Deuteronomy 26:1-11
Psalm 91:9-16
Romans 10:8b-13
Luke 4:1-13

First reading - virtual consensus. The first several verses serve to preserve the liturgical setting, which is completed by verse 11. This passage gives direction for offerings in response to God who is Lord of history and nature. The psalm expresses trust in the Lord who protects his people. Second reading - virtual consensus. This versification begins the passage with "The word is near you." Verses 5-8a contain an unnecessary rabbinical discourse whose argumentation would not be easily understood. Third reading - consensus.

Second Sunday of Lent

Genesis 15:1-12, 17-18
Psalm 127
Philippians 3:17-4:1
Luke 13:31-35
or Luke 9:28-36

First reading - near consensus. By beginning with verse 1, the whole passage is presented in the "oracle of salvation" style (i.e, the proclamation to fear not, the reasons, and the results). This provides the childless setting in which God's promise is made, as well as a liturgical introduction for homiletic purposes. The psalm affirms that "sons are a heritage from the Lord." Second reading-consensus. Luke 9:28-36 is provided as an alternative for those Churches that wish to maintain the tradition of reading a transfiguration gospel on this Sunday.

Third Sunday of Lent

Exodus 3:1-15
Psalm 103:1-13
1 Corinthians 10:1-13
Luke 13:1-9

First reading - virtual consensus. This uses the most comprehensive versification for ease of reading. This passage gives the call of Moses. The psalm is an exhortation to praise God for his goodness, with a reference to God making his ways known to Moses. Second reading - virtual consensus. Third reading - consensus.

Fourth Sunday of Lent

Joshua 5:9-12
Psalm 34:1-8
2 Corinthians 5:16-21
Luke 15:1-3, 11-32

First reading - near consensus. Isaiah 12:2-6 appears as the canticle in lieu of a psalm at Advent 3-C. The Josua passage gives an account of the transition of God's people from nourishment by manna to nourishment from the produce of the land of Canaan. The psalm gives praise for God's goodness and ends with the words, "O taste and see that the Lord is good." Second reading - near consensus. This passage should begin with verse 16. 1 Corinthians 1:18-31 now appears at Epiphany 4-A, Tuesday of Holy Week, and Holy Cross (1:18-24). Third reading - virtual consensus. Because the gospel is lengthy, verses 1-3 are included for contextual orientation.

Fifth Sunday of Lent

Isaiah 43:16-21
Psalm 126
Philippians 3:8-14
John 12:1-8

First reading - consensus. This passage gives God's promise to restore his people from Babylon. The psalm is a song of thanks for deliverance. Second reading - consensus. None of the gospel readings for this Sunday in the various lectionaries related well either to the first or to the second readings. The John 12 passage is a good one as a Johannine prefiguration of the passion, one that portrays the involvement of the women.

Lent 6 (when observed as Palm Sunday) (A, B,C)

See explanatory notes under Year A

Lent 6 (when observed as Passion Sunday) (A, B,C)

See explanatory notes under Year A

Monday, Tuesday, Wednesday of Holy Week (A,B,C)

See explanatory notes under Year A

Holy Thursday (A,B,C)

See explanatory notes under Year A

Good Friday (A, B,C)

See explanatory notes under Year A

Easter Vigil (A,B,C)

See explanatory notes under Year A

Easter (A, B,C)

See explanatory notes under Year A

Easter Evening (A,B,C)

See explanatory notes under Year A

Second Sunday of Easter
                                         Acts 5:27-32
Psalm 2
Revelation 1:4-8
John 20:19-31

Although this Acts passage appeared at Easter 3-C in two lectionaries, it was decided to use it here because it is kerygmatic and complements both the second reading and gospel with its resurrection appearance. In this passage the authorities question the apostles' teaching. Peter's response is, "We must obey God." The psalm breathes the same spirit: "Why do the nations conspire," and "I will tell of the decreee of the Lord." The second reading was slightly altered, in accord with several of the lectionaries, to include the important proclamation of the titles of the risen Lord. These titles relate the reading directly to the first reading and to the gospel. The sequential reading of Revelation is nonetheless maintained. Third reading - near consenses. John 21:1-14 appears at Easter 3-C.

Third Sunday of Easter
                                         Acts 9:1-20
Psalms 30:4-12
Revelation 5:11-14
John 21:1-19
    or John 21:15-19

The Acts passage appears in several lectionaries on this Sunday. This narration of the conversion of Saul does not appear elsewhere in the Sunday lectionary, only on the feast of Peter and Paul. It complements the apostolic commissioning of Peter in the gospel. The psalm is a thanksgiving for healing and deliverance from false security to true security in God. Second reading - virtual consensus. Third reading - consensus.

Fourth Sunday of Easter
                                       Acts 13:15-16, 26-33
Psalm 23
Revelation 7:9-17
John 10:22-30

This section of Acts 13 appeared in several lectionaries. The emphasis in the Acts reading during these Sundays should be more on kerygmatic preaching and less on narrative. The speech in verses 26-33 forms the heart of this section. The psalm is related to the gospel and its theme of the good shepherd. Second reading - virtual consensus. Third reading - virtual consensus. Verses 22-26 are used in several lectionaries. They give the fuller context of the reading.

Fifth Sunday of Easter

Acts 14:8-18
Psalm 145:13b-21
Revelation 21:1-6
John 13:31-35

The first reading is a powerful healing and preaching passage that avoids the anti-Semitic material in Acts 14:19-28 and Acts 13:44-52. In this first reading Paul and Barnabas are hailed as gods for healing the man at Lystra. The psalm directs praise to the Lord for his goodness. Second reading - near consensus. Verse 6 provides a good ending. Third reading - consensus. In the context verse 33b is seen to refer to all, not just Jews.

Sixth Sunday of Easter

Acts 15:1-2, 22-29
Psalm 67
Revelation 21:10, 22-27
John 14:23-29

The Acts 15 passage appears in several lectionaries. Acts 14:8-18 appears on the previous Sunday. In the first reading Paul preaches in Athens on Mar's Hill. The psalm in one of praise that contains the invitation, "Come and hear, all you who fear God, and I will tell what he has done for me." Second reading - virtual consensus. The visual detail of verses 11-14 was considered unhelpful for most congregations. Verses 22-27 seemed integral to the passage, containing many images that complement the experience during the Easter season of catechumens and the newly - baptized (e.g., the Book of Life). Third reading consensus.

Ascension (A,B,C)
See explanatory notes under Year A

Seventh Sunday of Easter

Acts 16:16-34
Psalm 97
Revelation 22:12-14, 16-17, 20
John 17:20-26

The Acts 16 passage appears in several lectionaries. Verses 16-34 show the bondage of Paul and Silas resulting from their freeing the slave girl from her bondage. Acts 7:55-59 now appears at Easter 5-A. The psalm expresses the confidence that the Lord delivers his saints from the wicked. Second reading - virtual consensus. Verse 20 is an excellent ending to the readings from Revelation and to the Easter season. Third reading consensus.

Pentecost (A,B,C)
See explanatory notes under Year A

Trinity Sunday

Proverbs 8:22-31
Psalm 8

Romans 5:1-5
John 16:12-15

First reading - near consensus. Isaiah 6:1-8 appears at Epiphany 5-C. In the Proverbs passage, Wisdom speaks as a prophetess, having been with God from the time of creation. The psalm proclaims God's glory as seen in creation and for honoring humanity as a part of that creation. The Romans 5 passage appears in several lectionaries. 1 Peter 1:3-9 appears at Easter 2-A. Third reading - near consensus. John 20:19-23 appears at Pentecost A.

Proper 4   1 Kings 8:22-23, 41-43
                                             Psalm 100
                                             Galatians 1:1-10
                                             Luke 7:1-10

With this first reading Year C begins its semi-continuous treatment of 1 and 2 Kings, the Elijah - Elisha narrative. These selections begin with Solomon's dedication of the Temple and conclude with Elisha's death. For a further explanation of the semi-continuous material, see the introduction, pp. 18-25. This passage from 1 Kings 8 depicts Solomon's dedication of the Temple and includes his petition to God to hear the prayer of the foreigner that all may know God. The psalm is a hymn calling on all nations to bless the Lord. Second reading - consensus. Third reading - consensus.

Proper 5   1 Kings 17:17-24
                                             Psalm 113
                                             Galatians 1:11-24
                                             Luke 7:11-17

In the first reading, Elijah returns life to the son of the widow. The psalm is a hymn celebrating the Lord as the helper of the humble, "he raises the poor from the dust, and lifts the needy from the ash heap." Second reading - virtual consensus. Verses 20-24 serve to bring the reference back to Paul's original persecution of the Church and to his present ministry, which brings praise to God. Third reading - consensus.

Proper 6   1 Kings 19:1-8
                                             Psalm 42
                                             Galatians 2:15-21
                                             Luke 7:36-8:3

The first reading depicts Elijah fleeing for his life and being ministered to by an angel of the Lord. The psalm expresses the need for hope in God, though momentarily "cast down." Second reading - virtual consensus. Verses 11-14 are not the real point of the passage. Exclusion of them also serves to avoid the scholarly disagreement as to whether or not verses 15-21 contain Paul's continuing discourse with Peter. Third reading - virtual consensus. Verses 1-3 of chapter 8 introduce two important matters: (a) one of Luke's important summary statements (verse 1 a) and (b) explicit recognition of the women who followed Jesus.

Proper 7

1 Kings 19:9-14
Psalm 43
Galatians 3:23-29
Luke 9:18-24

In the first reading a discouraged Elijah hides in a cave where he hears the still, small voice of God. The psalm is a prayer for vindication containing the same refrain as psalm 42 on the preceding Sunday, "Why are you cast down, O my soul?" Second reading virtual consensus. Verses 23-25 preserve the Pauline doctrine of justification by grace. Third reading - consensus.

Proper 8

1 Kings 19:15-21
Psalm 44:1-8
Galatians 5:1, 13-25
Luke 9:51-62

In the first reading Elijah is instructed to return to Jerusalem, and the call of Elisha is issued. The psalm is a part of a prayer for deliverance from enemies, and it contains an acknowledgment of God's past mercies. Second reading - virtual consenses. Verses 19-25 help provide parallel lists of self-indulgence and fruits of the Spirit. These verses include, "there can be no law against things like that." Third reading - consensus.

Proper 9

1 Kings 21:1-3, 17-21
Psalm 5:1-8
Galatians 6:7-18
Luke 10:1-12, 17-20

The first reading gives the account of Ahab coveting and taking Naboth's vineyard, and God's judgment on this. The psalm is a prayer for deliverance from personal enemies. God is confessed as the one who hates wickedness and who blesses the righteous. Second reading - virtual consensus. Verses 7 - 10 give a summary of verses 1-5 and provide a more striking beginning than the earlier verses. Verses 17-18 are Gospel material about the cross and deserve inclusion. Third reading - virtual consensus.

Proper 10

2 Kings 2:1, 6-14
Psalm 139:1-12
Colossians 1:1-14
Luke 10:25-37

The first reading depicts the ascension of Elijah and the transfer of his office to Elisha. The psalm is a prayer acknowledging that God is not bound by any limitations, but knows all and is present everywhere. In the second reading verses 15-20 are not included since they appear at Proper 29 (Christ the King), Year C. Third reading - consensus.

Proper 11

2 Kings 4:8-17
Psalm 139:13-18
Colossians 1:21-29
Luke 10:38-42

The first reading tells of Elisha's promise of a son to a barren woman and the fulfillment of that promise. The psalm acknowledges God's continuing creation through the gift of life. Second reading - virtual consensus. Verses 21-23 portray some of the humanity of Paul as servant, which is neatly rounded out by verse 29. Third reading - consensus.

Proper 12

2 Kings 5:1-15ab
Psalm 21:1-7
Colossians 2:6-15
Luke 11:1-13

Their first reading depicts the cure of Naaman's leprosy and his recognition of the God of Israel. The psalm is one of thanksgiving in which God is praised for having answered prayer. Second reading - virtual consenses. Third reading - consensus.

Proper 13

2 Kings 13:14-20a
Psalm 28
Colossians 3:1-11
Luke 12:13-21

The first reading contains the death of Elisha. The psalm is a prayer for help and expresses assurance of an answer. Second reading - virtual consenses. Third reading - consensus.

Proper 14

Jeremiah 18:1-11
Psalm 14
Hebrews 11:1-3, 8-19
Luke 12:32-40

With this Sunday Year C begins readings from the major and minor prophets. This passage from Isaiah is the allegory of the potter and the clay in which God says that, like the potter, he would destroy the spoiled and shape anew. But the people would not listen. The psalm is a description of the wicked, ending with a longing cry for better times. Second reading - virtual consensus. This selection of verses puts the emphasis on faith, creation, and Abraham as a man of faith. Third reading - virtual consensus. Verse 32 provides a good eschatological setting for the beginning of the passage.

Proper 15   Jeremiah 20:7-13
                                                 Psalm 10:12-18
                                                 Hebrews 12:1-2, 12-17
                                                 Luke 12:49-56

In the first reading Jeremiah complains to the Lord yet must nonetheless proclaim the Lord. The psalm is a prayer for relief expressing the confidence that an answer will come. Second reading - virtual consensus. Verses 1-2 introduce verses 12-17. The intervening verses on discipline were omitted because they reflect a male-dominated society. Third reading - virtual consensus. Verses 54-56 provide a good ending, especially because of the cloud image.

Proper 16   Jeremiah 28:1-9
                                                 Psalm 84
                                                 Hebrews 12:18-29
                                                 Luke 13:22-30

The first reading depicts Jeremiah's confrontation of the false prophet Hananiah. The psalm is an expression of longing to be in the presence of God and of trust that God will hear such a prayer. Second reading - this selection continues the in-course reading of this chapter. The preceding verses were read on the previous Sunday. Third reading - consensus.

Proper 17   Ezekiel 18:1-9, 25-29
                                                 Psalm 15
                                                 Hebrews 13:1-8
                                                 Luke 14:1, 7-14

In the first reading the word is given that the sinner will die, but the righteous will live. Yet the people complain that this is not just. The psalm describes the security of those whose lives are faithful to the Lord. Second reading - this selection continues the incourse reading. The preceding verses were read on the previous Sunday. Third reading - consensus.

Proper 18   Ezekiel 33:1-11
                                                 Psalm 94:12-22
                                                 Philemon 1-20
                                                 Luke 14:25-33

In the first reading Ezekiel is called to be Israel's watchman, one who warns against wickedness. The psalm is an expression of confidence in the faithfulness of the Lord, who protects against the wicked. Second reading - virtual consensus. Since this is a short book, all of the significant verses are included. Third reading - consensus.

Proper 19   Hosea 4:1-3, 5:15-6:6
                                                 Psalm 77:11-20

1 Timothy 1:12-17
Luke 15:1-10

The first reading gives a description of the sins of the people which lead them away from God and gives the prescription for their return, "I desire steadfast love, not sacrifice". The psalm recites the deeds by which God has shown himself partial to this people. Second reading - consensus. Third reading - virtual consensus. Verses 11-32 now appear at Lent 4-C.

Proper 20   Hosea 11:1-11
                                            Psalm 107:1-9
                                            1 Timothy 2:1-7
                                            Luke 16:1-13

In the first reading the Lord is pictured as a loving father who chastises a disobedient child. His compassion restrains his anger. The psalm is a thanksgiving to the Lord for his goodness, as seen in his wonderful deeds. Second reading - consensus. Verse 8 unnecessary because it introduces a new thought and makes a rubrical point. Third reading - consensus.

Proper 21   Joel 2:23-30
                                            Psalms 107:1, 33-43
                                            1 Timothy 6:6-19
                                            Luke 16:19-31

The first reading indicates that after the plague of locusts the Lord will satisfy his people with plenty and help them to know that he is God, who pours out his Spirit on all. The psalm is one of thanksgiving, particularly for the blessing of the earth. Second reading - virtual consensus. This passage corresponds well to the story of the rich man and Lazarus in the gospel. Third reading - consensus.

Proper 22   Amos 5:6-7, 10-15
                                            Psalm 101
                                            2 Timothy 1:1-14
                                            Luke 17:5-10

The first reading is a call to repentance. It appears in several lectionaries at Proper 23B. It details specific sins and urges that we "seek good, and not evil, hate evil, and love good." The psalm is a profession of integrity. Second reading - virtual consensus. This selection incorporates the apostolic greeting and the personal touch of Paul in mentioning individual names. Third reading - virtual consensus. Verses 1-4 are not necessary and would only create a long reading in addition to an already lengthy second reading.

Proper 23   Micah 1:2, 2:1-10
                                            Psalm 26

2 Timothy 2:8-15
Luke 17:11-19

The first reading is a description of the wickedness of the people despite the work of the Lord. The psalm is a prayer for deliverance and for integrity in the face of wickedness. Second reading - virtual consensus. Several lectionaries begin at verse 8. Third reading - consensus.

Proper 24

Habakkuk 1:1-3, 2:1-4
Psalm 119:137-144
2 Timothy 3:14-4:5
Luke 18:1-8

The first reading appears in all of the lectionaries at Proper 22-C. In it the prophet asks why he must see so much evil. God's answer is for patience, for "the righteous shall live by his faith." The psalm is an acknowledgment of the Lord's justice. Second reading - virtual consensus. Third reading - consensus.

Proper 25

Zephaniah 3:1-9
Psalm 3
2 Timothy 4:6-8, 16-18
Luke 18:9-14

The first reading gives the sins of the people and promises the Lord's action. The psalm is a prayer for protection in evil, expressing confidence in the Lord. Second reading - consenses. Third reading - consensus.

Proper 26

Haggai 2:1-9
Psalm 65:1-8
2 Thessalonians 1:5-12
Luke 19:1-10

The first reading provides good eschatological material for the end of the liturgical year and has the same theme as the gospel. In this passage is contained the promise of a new temple to replace the one in ruins. The psalm tells of the goodness of gathering at the temple to sing God's praise. By beginning the second reading at verse 5 the eschatological theme of the passage is kept without the problem of the delay of the parousia. The passage does not go through 2:2 since this is the introduction to the next section. Third reading - consensus.

Proper 27

Zechariah 7:1-10
Psalm 9:11-20
2 Thessalonians 2:13-3:5
Luke 20:27-38

In answer to an inquiry about fasting, the first reading indicates that the Lord would rather have kindness and mercy. The psalm is a prayer for help ending with an assurance of and a prayer for justice. Second reading - near consensus. Third reading - consensus.

Verses 28-33 are necessary to Jesus' words on marriage in the context of the resurrection.

Proper 28   Malachi 4:1-6 (3:19-24 in Hebrew)
                                        Psalm 82
                                        2 Thessalonians 3:6-13
                                        Luke 21:5-19

The first reading suits well the eschatological nature of this part of the calendar. It is a description of the day of judgment and the promise of one who will turn hearts. The psalm is a plea for God to judge the earth. Second reading - near consensus. Third reading - consensus.

Proper 29   2 Samuel 5:1-5
(Christ the King)   Psalm 95
                                        Colossians 1:11-20
                                        John 12:9-19

In the first reading David is made king of Israel. Jeremiah 23:1-6 appears at Christ the King, Year B. The psalm is a song of praise of the Lord," a great King above all gods." Second reading - virtual consensus. Third reading - this selection draws on the old tradition of association between Palm Sunday material and the First Sunday of Advent for which there is much hymnody. Luke 23:35-43 is included in the gospel on Palm/Passion Sunday. This passage has as its primary theme the pathos of the crucified criminal, not the exaltation of Christ as king. Jesus as Pantocrator is a theme not available in Luke. By concluding the John 12 passage at verses 18 and 19 the triumphal entry is referred back to the raising of Lazarus, and the universal dimension of Christ's reign is emphasized ("all the world is running after him").

Special Days

Thanksgiving Day

Deuteronomy 8:7-18
Psalm 65
2 Corinthians 9:6-15
Luke 17:11-19

Joel 2:21-27
Psalm 126
1 Timothy 2:1-7
Matthew 6:25-33

Deuteronomy 26:1-11
Psalm 100
Philippians 4:4-9
John 6:25-35

These lessons were drawn from several of the lectionaries and are not tied to any of the three years of the lectionary.

All Saints
(November 1 or the first
Sunday in November)

A.   Revelation 7:9-17
Psalm 34:1-10
1 John 3:1-3
Matthew 5:1-12

The readings for All Saints were drawn from several of the lectionaries. The first reading gives the vision of all those in heaven who have served God through tribulation. The psalm praises God for his goodness in giving deliverance from trouble. The second reading relates well to the Revelation passage. Second reading - near consensus. Third reading - consensus.

B.   Revelation 21:1-6a.
Psalm 24:1-6
Colossians 1:9-14
John 11:32-44

The first reading pairs well with the Lazarus gospel. It contains the vision of the new heaven and the new earth. The psalm is an acknowledgment that the earth is the Lord's, and this determines the character of God's people.

C.   Daniel 7:1-3, 15-18
Psalm 149

Ephesians 1:11-23
Luke 6:20-36

The first reading is not used elsewhere in the lectionary. It is a good text for this day and it pairs well with the gospel. It gives Daniel's dream of the four beasts and the explanation of the dream. The psalm is an exhortation to praise God, who takes pleasure in his people and adorns the humble with victory.

Annunciation (A,B,C)
(March 25)

Isaiah 7:10-14
Psalm 45 or 40:6-10
Hebrews 10:4-10
Luke 1:26-38

The first reading speaks of the young woman who will give birth to Emmanuel. Psalm 45 is a description of a royal wedding. Psalm 40 is a song expressing grateful obedience. Second reading - near consensus. This passage from Hebrews is especially appropriate when the Annunciation precedes Holy Week. Beginning with verse 4 serves to give the context for the argument and avoids the difficult beginning with "Consequently" in verse 5. Third reading - consensus

Visitation (A,B,C)
(May 31)

1 Samuel 2:1-10
Psalm 113
Romans 12:9-16b
Luke 1:39-57

In the first reading the song of Hannah, which includes the Canticle of Mary, parallels the gospel. The psalm is a hymn celebrating the Lord as the helper of the humble. Second reading - near consensus. Colossians 3:12-17 appears now at First Sunday after Christmas, Year C. Third reading - virtual consensus. The inclusion of verses 48-57 presents the Canticle of Mary and provides a Marian rather than Advent emphasis.

Presentation (A,B,C)
(February 2)

Malachi 3:1-4
Psalm 84 or 24:7-10
Hebrews 2:14-18
Luke 2:22-40

The first reading contains the promise that God will send his messenger to prepare the day of judgment. Psalm 84 gives praise for the temple as a place to experience the presence of the living God. Psalm 24 is part of a liturgy used when entering the sanctuary. Second reading - consensus. Third reading - consensus.

Holy Cross (A,B,C)
(September 14)

Numbers 21:4b-9
Psalm 98:1-5 or 78:1-2, 34-38

1 Corinthians 1:18-24
John 3:13-17

In the first reading the fiery serpents afflict the complaining people, and the bronze serpent is lifted up to protect them. Psalm 98 is a victory song with a summons to praise. Psalm 78 opens with a reference to a parable, which is the way the serpent incident is used in the gospel, then refers to the goodness of God in sparing his faithless people. Second reading - particularly appropriate with first and third readings. Third reading - this parallels the theme of "lifting up" in the first reading.

Index of Scripture Readings

(Versification follows that of the *Revised Standard Version*)

Deuteronomy

4:32-40	Trinity Sunday, A
6:1-9	Proper 26, B
8:1-10	January 1, A (New Year)
8:7-18	Thanksgiving Day, A
18:15-20	4th Sunday after Epiphany, B
26:1-11	Lent 1, C
26:1-11	Thanksgiving Day, C
30:15-20	6th Sunday after Epiphany, A (first option)
34:1-12	Proper 23, A

Josua

5:9-12	Lent 4, C

Judges

None

Ruth

1:1-19a	Proper 24, A
2:1-13	Proper 25, A
4:7-17	Proper 26, A

1 Samuel

2:1-10	Visitation (May 31)
2:18-20, 26	First Sunday after Christmas, C (first option)
3:1-10, (11-20)	2nd Sunday after Epiphany, B
16:1-13	Lent 4, A
16:1-13	Proper 4, B
16:14-23	Proper 5, B

2 Samuel

1:1, 17-27	Proper 6, B
5:1-5	Proper 29, C
5:1-12	Proper 7, B

6:1-15	Proper 8, B
7:1-17	Proper 9, B
7:8-16	Advent 4, B
7:18-29	Proper 10, B
11:1-15	Proper 11, B
12:1-14	Proper 12, B
12:15b-24	Proper 13, B
18:1, 5, 9-15	Proper 14, B
18:24-33	Proper 15, B
23:1-7	Proper 16, B

1 Kings

2:1-4, 10-12	Proper 17, B
8:22-23, 41-43	Proper 4, C
17:8-16	Proper 27, B
17:17-24	Proper 5, C
19:1-8	Proper 6, C
19:9-14	Proper 7, C
19:15-21	Proper 8, C
21:1-3, 17-21	Proper 9, C

2 Kings

2:1-12 a	Last Sunday after Epiphany, B (Transfiguration)
2:1, 6-14	Proper 10, C
4:8-17	Proper 11, C
5:1-14	6th Sunday after Epiphany, B
5:1-15 ab	Proper 12, C
13:14-20 a	Proper 13, C

1 Chronicles

NONE

2 Chronicles   (112 Psalms used)

36:14-23	Lent 4, B

Ezra

NONE

Nehemiah

8:1-4a, 5-6, 8-10   3rd Sunday after
Epiphany, C

Tobit

NONE

Judith

NONE

Esther

NONE

1 Maccabees

NONE

2 Maccabees

NONE

Job

7:1-7   5th Sunday after Epiphany, B

28:20-28   Proper 20, B

42:1-6   Proper 21, B

Psalms

See Psalm Table

Proverbs

2:1-8   Proper 18, B (second option)

8:22-31   Trinity Sunday, C

22:1-2, 8-9   Proper 19, B

Ecclesiastes

2:1-13   January 1, B (New Year)

Song of Solomon (Song of Songs)

NONE

Wisdom

NONE

Ecclesiasticus (Sirach)

3:3-7, 14-17   First Sunday after
Christmas, C (second option)

5:8-15   Proper 18, B (first option)

15:15-20   6th Sunday after Epiphany, A
(second option)

24:1-4, 12-16   Second Sunday after
Christmas (second option)

27:4-7   8th Sunday after Epiphany, C
(first option)

Isaiah

2:1-5   Advent 1, A

6:1-8   Trinity Sunday, B

6:1-8 (9-13)   5th Sunday after
Epiphany, C

7:10-14   Annunciation (March 25)

7:10-16   Advent 4, A

9:1-4   3rd Sunday after Epiphany, A

9:2-7   Christmas, First Proper

11:1-10   Advent 2, A

12:2-6   Canticle in lieu of psalm
Advent 3, C; Easter Vigil

25:6-9   Easter B (lesson 1, second
option)

35:1-10   Advent 3, A

40:1-11   Advent 2, B

42:1-9   Baptism of the Lord, A, (1st
Sunday after Epiphany)

42:1-9   Holy Week, Monday

43:16-21   Lent 5, C

43:18-25   7th Sunday after
Epiphany, B

44:1-8   Pentecost, A (second option)

49:1-7   2nd Sunday after Epiphany, A

49:1-7   Holy Week, Tuesday

49:1-10   January 1, C (New Year)

49:8-13   7th Sunday after Epiphany, A

50:4-9a   Lent 6, A, B, C (Palm Sunday)

50:4-9a   Lent 6, A, B, C (Passion Sunday)

50:4-9a   Holy Week, Wednesday

52:7-10   Christmas, Third Proper

52:13-53:12   Good Friday

53:7-12   Proper 24, B

54:5-14   Easter Vigil

55:1-11   Easter Vigil

55:10-13   8th Sunday after Epiphany, C (second option)

58:3-9a   5th Sunday after Epiphany, A

60:1-6   Epiphany

61:1-4   Baptism of the Lord, C (1st Sunday after Epiphany)

61:1-4, 8-11   Advent 3, B

61:10-62:3   First Sunday after Christmas, B

62:1-5   2nd Sunday after Epiphany, C

62:6-7, 10-12   Christmas, Second Proper

63:7-9   First Sunday after Christmas, A

63:16-64:8   Advent 1, B

65:17-25   Easter C (lesson 1, second option)

Jeremiah

1:4-10   4th Sunday after Epiphany, C

17:5-10   6th Sunday after Epiphany, C

18:1-11   Proper 14, C

20:7-13   Proper 15, C

23:1-6   Proper 29, B (Christ the King)

28:1-9   Proper 16, C

31:1-6   Easter A (lesson 1, second option)

31:7-9   Proper 25, B

31:7-14   Second Sunday after Christmas (first option)

31:31-34   Lent 5, B

31:31-34   Holy Thursday, C

33:14-16   Advent 1, C

Lamentations

NONE

Baruch

3:9-15, 32-4:4   Easter Vigil

5:1-9   Advent 2, C (first option)

Ezekiel

18:1-9, 25-29   Proper 17, C

33:1-11   Proper 18, C

34:11-16, 20-24   Proper 29, A (Christ the King)

36:24-28   Easter Vigil

37:1-14   Lent 5, A

37:1-14   Pentecost B (second option) Easter Vigil

Daniel

7:1-3, 15-18   All Saints, C (Nov. 1)

7:9-14   Proper 28, B

12:1-3   Easter Evening (lesson 1, second option)

Hosea

2:14-20   8th Sunday after Epiphany, B

4:1-3, 5:15-6:6   Proper 19, C

11:1-11   Proper 20, C

Joel

2:1-2, 12-17 a   Ash Wednesday

2:21-27   Thanksgiving Day, B

2:23-30   Proper 21, C

Amos

5:6-7, 10-15   Proper 22, C

5:18-24   Proper 27, A

Obadiah

NONE

Jonah

3:1-5, 10   3rd Sunday after Epiphany, B

Micah

1:2; 2:1-10   Proper 23, C

5:2-5a   Advent 4, C

6:1-8   4th Sunday after Epiphany, A

Nahum

NONE

Habakkuk

1:1-3, 2:1-4   Proper 24, C

Zephaniah

1:7, 12-18   Proper 28, A

3:1-9   Proper 25, C

3:14-20   Advent 3, C; Easter Vigil

Haggai

2:1-9   Proper 26, C

Zechariah

7:1-10   Proper 27, C

Malachi

3:1-4   Advent 2, C (second option)

3:1-4   Presentation, (Feb. 2)

4:1-6   Proper 28, C (3:19-24 in Hebrew)

Matthew

1:18-25   Advent 4, A

2:1-12   Epiphany

2:13-15, 19-23   First Sunday after Christmas, A

3:1-12   Advent 2, A

3:13-17   Baptism of the Lord, A (1st. Sunday after Epiphany)

4:1-11   Lent 1, A

4:12-23   3rd Sunday after Epiphany, A

5:1-12   4th Sunday after Epiphany, A

5:1-12   All Saints, A (November 1)

5:13-16   5th Sunday after Epiphany, A

5:17-26   6th Sunday after Epiphany, A

5:27-37   7th Sunday after Epiphany, A

5:38-48   8th Sunday after Epiphany, A

6:1-6, 16-21   Ash Wednesday

6:25-33   Thanksgiving Day, B

7:21-29   Proper 4, A

9:9-13   Proper 5, A

9:14-17   January 1, B (New Year)

9:35-10:8   Proper 6, A

10:24-33   Proper 7, A

10:34-42   Proper 8, A

11:2-11   Advent 3, A

11:25-30   Proper 9, A

13:1-9, 18-23   Proper 10, A

13:24-30, 36-43   Proper 11, A

13:44-52   Proper 12, A

14:13-21   Proper 13, A

14:22-33   Proper 14, A

15:21-28   Proper 15, A

16:13-20   Proper 16, A

16:21-28   Proper 17, A

17:1-9   Lent 2, A (second option)

Mark

Luke

John

Acts

8:14-17 Baptism of the Lord, C (1st. Sunday after Epiphany)

8:26-40 Easter 5, B

9:1-20 Easter 3, C

10:34-43 Baptism of the Lord, A (1st Sunday after Epiphany)

10:34-43 Easter, A, B, C (lesson 1, first option); (Lesson 2, second option)

10:44-48 Easter 6, B

13:15-16, 26-33 Easter 4, C

14:8-18 Easter 5, C

15:1-2, 22-29 Easter 6, C

16:16-34 Easter 7, C

17:22-31 Easter 6, A

19:1-7 Baptism of the Lord, B (1st Sunday after Epiphany)

Romans

1:1-7 Advent 4, A

3:21-28 Proper 4, A

4:1-5, (6-12), 13-17 Lent 2, A

4:13-18 Proper 5, A

4:16-25 Lent 2, B

5:1-5 Trinity Sunday, C

5:1-11 Lent 3, A

5:6-11 Proper 6, A

5:12-19 Lent 1, A

5:12-19 Proper 7, A

6:3-11 Proper 8, A; Easter Vigil

7:14-25a Proper 9, A

8:6-11 Lent 5, A

8:9-17 Proper 10, A

8:12-17 Trinity Sunday, B

8:14-17 Pentecost C (first option)

8:18-25 Proper 11, A

8:22-27 Pentecost B (first option)

8:26-30 Proper 12, A

8:31-39 Proper 13, A

9:1-5 Proper 14, A

10:8b-13 Lent 1, C

11:13-16, 29-32 Proper 15, A

11:33-36 Proper 16, A

12:1-13 Proper 17, A

12:9-16b Visitation, (May 31)

13:1-10 Proper 18, A

13:11-14 Advent 1, A

14:5-12 Proper 19, A

15:4-13 Advent 2, A

16:25-27 Advent 4, B

1 Corinthians

1:1-9 2nd Sunday after Epiphany, A

1:3-9 Advent 1, B

1:10-17 3rd. Sunday after Epiphany, A

1:18-24 Holy Cross (September 14)

1:18-31 4th Sunday after Epiphany, A

1:18-31 Holy Week, Tuesday

1:22-25 Lent 3, B

2:1-11 5th Sunday after Epiphany, A

3:1-9 6th Sunday after Epiphany, A

3:10-11, 16-23 7th Sunday after Epiphany, A

4:1-5 8th Sunday after Epiphany, A

5:6-8 Easter Evening (lesson 2, first option)

6:12-20 2nd Sunday after Epiphany, B

7:29-31 (32-35) 3rd Sunday after Epiphany, B

8:1-13 4th Sunday after Epiphany, B

9:16-23 5th Sunday after Epiphany, B

9:24-27 6th Sunday after Epiphany, B

10:1-13 Lent 3, C

4:1-9	Proper 23, A
4:4-9	Thanksgiving Day, C
4:4-13	Advent 3, C

Colossians

1:1-14	Proper 10, C
1:9-14	All Saints, B (November 1)
1:11-20	Proper 29, C (Christ the King)
1:21-29	Proper 11, C
2:1-7	January 1, B (New Year)
2:6-15	Proper 12, C
3:1-4	Easter A (lesson 2, first option)
3:1-11	Proper 13, C
3:12-17	First Sunday after Christmas, C

1 Thessalonians

1:1-10	Proper 24, A
2:1-8	Proper 25, A
2:9-13, 17-20	Proper 26, A
3:9-13	Advent 1, C
4:13-18	Proper 27, A
5:1-11	Proper 28, A
5:16-24	Advent 3, B

2 Thessalonians

1:5-12	Proper 26, C
2:13-3:5	Proper 27, C
3:6-13	Proper 28, C

1 Timothy

1:12-17	Proper 19, C
2:1-7	Thanksgiving Day, B
2:1-7	Proper 20, C
6:6-19	Proper 21, C

2 Timothy

1:1-14	Proper 22, C
2:8-15	Proper 23, C
3:14-4:5	Proper 24, C
4:6-8, 16-18	Proper 25, C

Titus

2:11-14	Christmas, First Proper
3:4-7	Christmas, Second Proper

Philemon

1-20	Proper 18, C

Hebrews

1:1-4, 2:9-11	Proper 22, B
1:1-12	Christmas, Third Proper
2:10-18	First Sunday after Christmas, A
2:14-18	Presentation, (February 2)
4:1-3, 9-13	Proper 23, B
4:14-16	Proper 24, B
4:14-16, 5:7-9	Good Friday
5:1-6	Proper 25, B
5:7-10	Lent 5, B
7:23-28	Proper 26, B
9:11-15	Holy Week, Monday
9:24-28	Proper 27, B
10:4-10	Annunciation, (March 25)
10:5-10	Advent 4, C
10:11-18	Proper 28, B
10:16-25	Holy Thursday, C
11:1-3, 8-19	Proper 14, C
12:1-2, 12-17	Proper 15, C
12:1-3	Holy Week, Wednesday
12:18-29	Proper 16, C
13:1-8	Proper 17, C

James

1:17-27   Proper 18, B

2:1-5, 8-10, 14-17   Proper 19, B

3:13-18   Proper 20, B

4:13-17, 5:7-11   Proper 21, B

5:7-10   Advent 3, A

1 Peter

1:3-9   Easter 2, A

1:17-23   Easter 3, A

2:2-10   Easter 5, A

2:19-25   Easter 4, A

3:13-22   Easter 6, A

3:18-22   Lent 1, B

4:12-14; 5:6-11   Easter 7, A

2 Peter

1:16-21   Last Sunday after Epiphany,
A (Transfiguration)

3:8-15a   Advent 2, B

1 John

1:1-2:2   Easter 2, B

3:1-3   All Saints, A (November 1)

3:1-7   Easter 3, B

3:18-24   Easter 4, B

4:7-12   Easter 5, B

5:1-6   Easter 6, B

5:9-13   Easter 7, B

2 John

NONE

3 John

NONE

Jude

NONE

Revelation

1:4-8   Easter 2, C

1:4b-8   Proper 29, B (Christ the King)

5:11-14   Easter 3, C

7:9-17   Easter 4, C

7:9-17   All Saints, A (November 1)

21:1-6a   January 1, A (New Year)

21:1-6a   All Saints, B (November 1)

21:1-6   Easter 5, C

21:10, 22-27   Easter 6, C

22:12-14, 16-17, 20   Easter 7, C

Index of Psalms

(Numbering and versification follow that of the *Revised Standard Version*)

Psalm 28. Proper 13 C

29. Baptism of the Lord ABC, Trinity B

30: 4-12, Easter 3 C; Easter Vigil

31: 9-16, Passion Sunday ABC; 1-8, Easter 5 A

32. Epiphany 6 B; Proper 12 B

33: 18-22, Lent 2 A; 1-12, Trinity A; 12-22 Proper 4 A; Easter Vigil

34: 1-8, Lent 4 C; 11-22, Proper 13 B; 1-10, All Saints A

35: 17-28, Proper 24 B

36: 5-10, Epiphany 2 C; 5-10, Monday in Holy Week

37: 1-11, Epiphany 4 A; 1-11, Epiphany 7 C

38.

39.

40: 1-11, Epiphany 2 A; 6-10, Annunciation (alt.)

41. Epiphany 7 B

42. Proper 6 C; Easter Vigil

43. Proper 7 C

44: 1-8, Proper 8 C

45. Annunciation ABC

46. Proper 6 A; Proper 6 B; Easter Vigil

47. Ascension ABC

48. Proper 7 B

49.

50: 1-6, Transfiguration B; 7-15, Proper 27 A

51: 1-12, Ash Wednesday ABC; 10-17, Lent 5 B

52.

53. Proper 11 B

54.

55.

56.

57. Proper 5 B

58.

59.

60.

61.

62: 5-12, Epiphany 3 B; 5-12, Epiphany 7 A

Psalm **63:** 1-8, Epiphany 2 B

64.

65: 1-8, Proper 26 C; Thanksgiving A

66: 8-20, Easter 6 A

67. Easter 6 C; Proper 16 B; January 1 (Name of Jesus) ABC

68: 1-10, Easter 7 A

69: 6-15, Proper 10 A

70. Wednesday in Holy Week

71: 1-6, Epiphany 4 C; 1-12, Tuesday in Holy Week

72: 1-8, Advent 2 A; 1-14, Epiphany ABC

73.

74.

75.

76. Proper 28 A

77: 11-20, Proper 19 C

78: 1-3, 10-20, Proper 15 A; 1-2, 34-38, Holy Cross (alt.)

79.

80: 1-7, Advent 1 B; 1-7, Advent 4 C

81: 1-10, Proper 22 A

82. Proper 28 C

83.

84. Proper 16 C; Presentation ABC

85: 8-13, Advent 2 B

86.

87.

88.

89: 1-4, 19-24, Advent 4 B; 20-37, Proper 9 B; 20-21, 24, 26, Holy Thursday "Chrism"

90: 1-12, Proper 23 B; 1-12, Janauary 1 C (New Year)

91: 9-16, Lent 1 C; 1-10, Proper 7 A

92: 1-4, 12-15, Epiphany 8 C

93. Christ the King B

94: 12-22, Proper 18 C

95. Lent 3 A; Proper 16 A; Christ the King C

96. Christmas

Psalm 131.

132: 11-18, Proper 10 B

133. Easter 2 B

134.

135: 1-14, Proper 23 A

136.

137: 1-6, Lent 4 B

138. Epiphany 5 C

139: 1-12, Proper 10 C; 13-18, Proper 11 C

140.

141.

142.

143: 1-10, Proper 13 A; 1-8, Proper 14 B; Easter Vigil

144.

145: 13b-21, Easter 5 C; 8-13, Proper 28 B

146: 5-10, Advent 3 A; Proper 27 B; Proper 24 A

147: 1-11, Epiphany 5 B; 12-20, Christmas 2 ABC

148.

149. All Saints C

150. Easter Evening

Sample Questionnaire

Name:_____

Community or Organization:_____

Position:_____

Address:_____

---

1. What is your normal function in public worship (for example, preacher/leader, reader, musician)?

   _____

2. What is your usual experience of the use of the lectionary? *Please circle.*
   1 Used every Sunday
   2 Used most Sundays
   3 Seldom used
   4 Other

   Comments:_____

   _____

3. If the lectionary is used in your congregation's worship, what lessons normally are read?
   1 All three lessons
   2 Two lessons
   3 One lesson. If one, which was usually chosen? (Please circle)
      a. Old Testament
      b. New Testament
      c. Gospel

   Comments:_____

   _____

4. What best describes the circumstances in which you evaluated the CCT Common Lectionary?
   1 Corporate worship
   2 Group study
   3 Private use or study
   4 Other

   Comments:_____

   _____

5. If this lectionary was evaluated through corporate worship, with what kind of congregation was this done? *Circle all that apply.*
   1 Parish
   2 Campus Ministry
      (College/University)
   3 Seminary
   4 Graduate Theological School
   5 Other

   Comments:_____

   _____

6. Over what period of time was this lectionary evaluated?
   1 Three years
   2 Two years

3 One year
4 Less than a year

Comments:_____

_____

7. For this evaluation, how many of the readings assigned to each day were used?
   1 Three
   2 Two
   3 One. If one, which was usually chosen? (Please circle)
      a. Old Testament
      b. New Testament
      c. Gospel

   Comments:_____

   _____

8. How often did you use the psalms contained in this lectionary?
   1 Never
   2 Occasionally
   3 Regularly

   Comments:_____

   _____

9. If you used the psalms either occasionally or regularly, how were they used? *Circle all that apply.*
   1 Unison reading
   2 Responsorial reading
   3 Read by one person to the congregation
   4 Sung by choir
   5 Sung responsorially by congregation
   6 Metrical texts sung
   7 Other

   Comments:_____

   _____

10. What is your overall response to the CCT Common Lectionary from a liturgical point of view (for example, calendar arrangement, suitabil-

ity of readings to seasons, etc.)?
   1 Very successful
   2 Moderately successful
   3 Unsuccessful
   4 No opinion

   Comments:_____

   _____

11. What is your overall response to this lectionary from a theological point of view (for example, coverage of the Scriptures, treatment of relationship between Old and New Testaments, etc.)?
   1 Very successful
   2 Moderately successful
   3 Unsuccessful
   4 No opinion

   Comments:_____

   _____

12. What is your overall reaction to this lectionary from a practical point of view (for example, length of readings, suitability of verses selected for readings, etc.)?
   1 Very successful
   2 Moderately successful
   3 Unsuccessful
   4 No opinion

   Comments:_____

   _____

13. From an ecumenical point of view, what is your reaction to the CCT Common Lectionary (for example, its incorporation of significant elements of your denominational lectionary; the kind of harmonization it has achieved of the various denominational lectionaries; etc.)?
   1 Very successful
   2 Moderately successful
   3 Unsuccessful
   4 No opinion

   Comments:_____

   _____

14. What is your overall reaction to the selection of readings for the Sundays following Pentecost in this lectionary?
    1 Very successful
    2 Moderately successful
    3 Unsuccessful
    4 No opinion

    Comments:_____

    _____

15. How would you evaluate the semi-continuous arrangement of readings from the Old Testament on the Sundays following Pentecost (for example, in terms of preaching and reading)?
    1 Very successful
    2 Moderately successful
    3 Unsuccessful
    4 No opinion

    Comments:_____

    _____

16. What do you judge to be the strength(s) of the CCT Common Lectionary?

_____

_____

_____

_____

17. What do you judge to be the weaknesses of the CCT Common Lectionary?

_____

_____

_____

_____

18. Please feel free to comment further. Should you wish to comment in detail on particular Sundays for feastdays (for example, assigned readings, versification, etc.), please consider using the following outline.

   Year A
   1. First Sunday of Advent—Last Sunday after Epiphany
   2. Ash Wednesday—Pentecost
   3. Trinity Sunday—Proper 29 (Sundays following Pentecost)

Year B

1. First Sunday of Advent—Last Sunday after Epiphany
2. Ash Wednesday—Pentecost
3. Trinity Sunday—Proper 29 (Sundays following Pentecost)

Year C

1. First Sunday of Advent—Last Sunday after Epiphany
2. Ash Wednesday—Pentecost
3. Trinity Sunday—Proper 29 (Sundays following Pentecost)

Completed questionnaires may be sent to denominational offices, for subsequent forwarding to the CCT, or directly to the secretariat of the CCT:

Consultation on Common Texts
1234 Massachusetts Avenue, N.W., Suite 1009
Washington, D.C. 20005